THE LOCATIONS

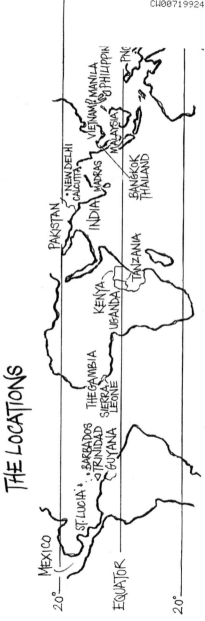

Through High Water and Low

AN UNUSUAL TRAVELLER

Margaret Haswell

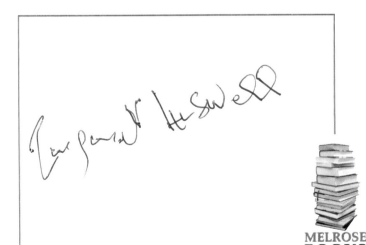

MELROSE
BOOKS

Published by

MELROSE BOOKS

An Imprint of Melrose Press Limited
St Thomas Place, Ely
Cambridgeshire
CB7 4GG, UK
www.melrosebooks.com

FIRST EDITION

Cover designed by Jeremy Kay

ISBN 978-1-907040-18-4

Printed and bound in Great Britain by:
CPI Anthony Rowe. Chuppenham, Wiltshire

Mixed Sources
Product group from well-managed forests and other controlled sources
www.fsc.org Cert no. SGS-COC-002953
© 1996 Forest Stewardship Council

Also by the same Author

Economics of Agriculture in a Savannah Village
The Changing Pattern of Economic Activity in a Gambia Village
Economics of Development in Village India
Potential for Economic Growth of Resource Development in Asian
Agriculture
Northeast Thailand
The Nature of Poverty
Energy for Subsistence
Tropical Farming Economics

Snake for Breakfast
Murder on Pawley's
Maria

For Shirley, again

ACKNOWLEDGEMENT

My grateful thanks to Robert Duncan for preparing maps and to Reg Moss for assistance with editing.

CONTENTS

ILLUSTRATIONS AND MAPS

FOREWORD

The *London Midland and Scottish* rail train steamed into Radlett station. A genial engine driver blew a whistle. Two small children looked up, scampered across the rail track and bolted into a carriage. They had been playing at the side of the track on their way to school; all dressed in navy blue blazers with white piping and panama hats. We were those children, I the elder, and we were inseparable, like twins. Even when we had to change schools and I had to cycle the seven-mile journey while my sister had to take the bus, she would let the bus go. She would wait on the roadside for me to cycle up. Then she would climb on the step fixed to the rear wheel of the bicycle and we would cycle to school together.

Shortly before my sister was twelve years old, she was admitted to a London hospital in the east end for an operation to remove her tonsils. Three weeks later, she was dead. She had contracted septicaemia. Instruments used on the previous patient had inadvertently not been sterilised before the operation on my sister.

Her death had left a family, shattered and broken.

PART ONE

CHAPTER 1

A NEW BEGINNING

Three years after Pam died, when I was seventeen, I bought a car for ten pounds with a gift of twenty-seven pounds from an aunt. It was a 1926 Morris coupe with an open back seat. It had one door on the passenger side and the battery sat on the running-board on the driver's side. I had bought the car from the cook at the Hertfordshire Institute of Agriculture where I was in my second year and was told by the Principal that I could not keep it on the premises. I threw up a scholarship and took a job on a farm.

I had been cruelly taken from school while in a remove for pupils selected for university entrance. My mother had suffered a total breakdown after Pam's death. My father had become unpredictable and given to wild fits of temper. He had become a victim of the Wall Street Crash of 1929. He had had to close *R. Haswell & Sons*, established over a hundred years earlier by his grandfather. Suddenly, against strongest pleas from my headmistress, he had taken me out of school and from home. I did not want to be doing what had been decided for me. I longed to be back at school. I had lost my friends.

Instead, I was on the payroll. The farmer and his family had had a dreadful tragedy. They kept a shop in the town and each week their son would drive to London and collect trays of pastries and cakes for sale in the shop. Two or three weeks before my arrival, blinded by the glare from the lights of an oncoming car, their son had driven into the back of a van and had been killed outright. The weekly fifty-mile journey to London had been handed over to me. There had been no driving tests at that time. It was a challenging experience.

But it had been the visits of an attractive young man, and our going out together in my car, which had worried this distressed family. They had not been able to accept that he was my first cousin, who happened to be working a few miles away. And, as we enjoyed each other's company, neither could we have known that war would soon change our lives, that he would become a bomber pilot, that he would be shot down on D-Day over Paris, and that he and his crew would all be killed.

After only nine months on the farm, I was sacked.

Post-First World War epitome of the jazz age, of good times, had come to an abrupt end with the 1926 general strike in Britain and the Wall Street Crash of 1929 in America. The roaring twenties had been ushered out and brought on the Great Depression. Yet, by the late nineteen-thirties, there had been a mood of optimism in Britain. People were going places. The good times were back.

I had left farming to pursue a career in journalism. I had taken a course in shorthand and aspired to become fluent in French. But I needed to save and I had gained an appointment as secretary to the portrait painter, Gerald Kelly, who had just returned to London from Southeast Asia. He had brought back coffin-like boxes of headdresses and costumes of Cambodian dancers, and numerous of his sketches and photographs which all had to be sorted. He had also appointed as his assistant, John Napper, a gangling young painter who was later to become a famous artist in his own right. While he and I were in Gerald's employ, Gerald was commissioned to paint the state portraits of King George VI and Queen Elizabeth. On their Majesties' visit to Gerald's studio, while the King and Gerald were busy talking in the hall, the Queen had slipped away and wandered into the room where I was working. I rose from my desk and curtsied. Then I saw what the Queen did not see, Gerald rush into the room and, behind the Queen, curtsy holding his arms out as though he wore a skirt. His dramatic entrance had been too late; had the Queen seen, she would have been greatly amused.

Life had become hectic in the Kelly household. Rarely could John or I leave work before late in the evening. There had been pressure to complete the Royal Portraits. Gerald had sent me to Buckingham Palace to collect the Crown Jewels.

"Don't take the same taxi back," he had said. And I had received from an inconspicuous side entrance to the Palace a small unidentified parcel wrapped in brown paper.

Then Gerald was elected President of the Royal Academy which added to the pressure, and Gerald's terrible temper became more frequent. He would throw hammers at his frame-maker, who would dart behind an easel for cover. And too often I would have to stand dressed in the very heavy royal robes while Gerald painted.

At the end of a year John had left but it had taken me another year before I had saved enough to study in France. Gerald had been surprisingly magnanimous. He knew Paris well. He had lived in the Latin Quarter, a haunt of painters and writers, and he had arranged for a friend at the University to teach me French. I packed a trunk with everything I possessed and gave notice to my landlady with whom I had had an attic room two streets from Gerald's studio, and I took the channel ferry to France prepared for a long stay.

It was late summer, 1939.

Chapter 2

New Directions

The Second World War was a long War which robbed a whole generation of their 'debutante' years. Young men and women, certain of their future as they set out on careers of their choice, found themselves drafted into the armed forces. Almost to the day Britain declared War on Germany, the unimaginable had been dismissed from their minds; the politicians had removed the threat of war which had hung over Europe as Adolf Hitler rose to power to become Germany's Dictator and self-styled *Fuhrer* of the German people. More than a year had passed since Hitler, nurturing national ambitions, had sent his armies into Austria; a conquest he had followed up by walking into Sudeten, a part of Czechoslovakia largely occupied by Germans. Hitler had promised to go no further in his territorial ambitions and an appeasement deal was signed. War had been averted.

But War had not been averted. On 24 August, 1939, Hitler signed a Treaty with Russia, setting alarm bells ringing throughout Europe. Next day, the British Government signed an Assistance Pact with Poland and requested Germany to withdraw her troops from that corridor of land which crucially lay between Germany and Russia.

One week later, on 2 September, 1939, Britain's Prime Minister, Neville Chamberlain, sent an ultimatum to Hitler to withdraw his troops from Poland by 11 o'clock on 3 September or Britain would have no alternative but to declare War on Germany.

As history records, there was no reply.

Sunday morning; and a stunned British public heard sirens blare across Britain. Nothing happened.

In those tense August days in England, I had settled in Paris and had started a course of study under an eminent French professor. With trunk and typewriter, I had found lodgings in Rue Vaneau for a stay of several months. There had been no panic, no hint of War, when I picked up an

English newspaper with the disturbing prediction of War with Germany. Yet all had been quiet in Paris and life was continuing its daily round. But not for much longer, it transpired. By a hair's-breadth as Britain declared War on Germany, all foreigners were told to leave Paris. With trunk and typewriter I was back crossing the channel, this time on a ferry carrying a full complement of worried English, going home to an uncertain future.

It had been a single plane that had strayed across the English Channel which had sparked off the sirens. No one knew what to do next; and the phrase 'the phoney War' was coined. The feared invasion had not happened.

In 1940, I answered an advertisement placed by Cambridge Flax, a private company under contract with the Ministry of Supply, for a woman who could drive. Flax from Belgium, the source of this natural fibre vital to the Armed Forces, had suddenly been cut off by Hitler's invasion of that country. Cambridge Flax, with an office in Cambridge, had one of the first of the Ministry's hurriedly commissioned flax factories half-built in Newmarket.

The Chairman of Cambridge Flax, known only as F.J. and believed to have links with Latin America, was an enigmatic man, yellow-complexioned with dark brown eyes and thick-set. He had a beautiful wife to whom he was devoted. But she was gravely ill, pallid and nervous. And it was my first task to drive her to wherever she wished to be taken.

Flax factories were being rushed up all over the country. "Where's the flax coming from to supply them?" said someone. "We don't grow it over here."

Two new sites in Yorkshire fell to F.J. – quite a distance from his Newmarket factory. Recalling that I had been at an agricultural college, he sent me, a lone traveller, to secure contracts from Yorkshire farmers for a total of 6,000 acres in time for the 1941 planting season – a tall order, as it turned out, as these traditionally cautious Yorkshire farmers would commit only about one or two acres to flax.

It was a bad winter that year. I had never visited Yorkshire before. All road signs had been removed to fool the Germans; black shades with slits to dim car headlights to avoid being seen by enemy aircraft did not help. Snowfall was heavy after Christmas and the car, fitted with snowshoes, floated over snow-capped roads like the surreal. Completely lost on one occasion during a snowstorm, I got out of the car and found it was perilously close to the River Ouse, within feet of plunging over the edge.

Miraculously, the target had been completed in time for planting. It remained only for the farmers to be supplied with the flax seed, which would soon flower into a breathtaking sea-mist of blue all across the county.

Foundations for the two factories had been laid – one at Easingwold north of York, the other in the Humber region at Howden by Boothferry Bridge.

"Which of the two Yorkshire factories would you like to manage?" F.J. had asked me.

While signing up contracts with farmers, I had discovered that Humberside had a history of flax growing where the high humidity produced excellent flax fibre. Without hesitation I said: "Howden." And F.J. found another woman to manage Easingwold.

F.J. had had 'a thing about women'. He had said: "A first-class woman is better than a second-class man." But all able-bodied men were rapidly being called up. And a German invasion of Britain was only a whisper away, just across the Channel.

Chapter 3

World at War

It had been over a year since the fall of France completed Germany's occupation of Western Europe and Hitler's attempt in a ferocious battle over Britain to destroy the fighters of the Royal Air Force and clear the way for invasion into England. Hitler's attempt had failed. The failure had been decisive. And so began England's long struggle alone.

Over Boothferry Bridge two miles down the road to Goole, Mr Hogan at the Labour Exchange was recruiting a thousand women for shift work in the Howden flax factory – women, many of whose husbands had been out of work for ten years during the depression of the 'thirties, women who in peacetime had been seasonal pea-pickers. The town buzzed with eager applicants. While right across the rural countryside of East and West Riding three thousand acres of flax had ripened.

Harvesters, machines hurriedly designed and not tested in the field, were distributed to all seventeen factories across England and Scotland. Humberside had its complement in place with operators raring to go. It was a national disaster. The pulling machines failed. They simply dug into the ground. The sun bore down on the standing crop which would shatter within days. Where would the seed for the next season come from or the fibre for vital webbing and aircraft fabric for the Armed Forces?

The Land Army was called in on a prayer. And, like a plague of locusts, they clean swept thousands of acres of standing flax – green-clad girls pulling the golden straw from the soil, bundling it into sheaves, defying the destructive rays of the sun.

The harvest had been saved.

And now the factory lorries were hauling in the flax from farms with the building still unfinished, gaping holes covered in black-out sheets; stack yard girls pitch forked the flax to the de-seeders on the factory floor.

In the manic situation of haste, one of the girls operating a de-seeder, annoyed by the safety guard, recklessly removed it. Down came the power-driven iron forks through her arms, pinning her to the de-seeder. She was a large girl and fortunately had only flesh wounds but it had terrified her and was a stark warning for our pea-picking novices on the factory floor.

During those desperate 1941 months for Britain engaged in fighting the German might, the Ministry of Supply had taken over all seventeen flax factories under the umbrella of Home Flax Production chaired by Lord De La Warr. F.J. had simply vanished and an overstretched female labour force was working a three-shift system around the clock seven days of the week; but men were needed for machinery maintenance. With all able-bodied men at the front, the Ministry had sent German prisoners-of-war under armed guard each day, a surly and unwilling complement to the work force who were soon withdrawn and replaced by Italian prisoners-of-war

Having in mind Humberside's famous history of flax growing, the Ministry had installed at the Howden factory retting tanks; the finest of our flax would be retted to produce high quality fibre urgently needed for aircraft production. It so happened that we had a large empty cottage on the factory site in which I had made available one room to a conscientious objector whom the Ministry had told us to employ. The women had objected to his presence on the factory floor with their husbands and brothers at the front; but he was a highly educated man and able to carry out research on which of our harvested flax should go to the retting tanks before being scutched and which scutched green straight from the field. The Italian prisoners-of-war were billeted on site in the available space at the cottage.

In the long dark weeks before Christmas, fieldsmen were out persuading farmers to commit 3,000 acres to flax for the 1942 planting season; when one of our most active fieldsmen, on returning home one evening in the failing light, did not see an iron rod sticking out from the back of a lorry in front of him. The rod went through his windscreen into his forehead and killed him instantly.

The loss of a fieldsman, a factory worker on sick leave, a

hold-up on the production line through an electrical fault, a worker distressed by bad news of a husband or a brother serving in the armed forces and the stream of telegrams from the Ministry calling urgently for ever more of our finest flax fibre used in building our fighter and bomber aircraft were some of the many pressures. Yet there was an abundance of good humour on the factory floor which, at times, bordered on farce such as when a German plane dropped a bomb which missed us. "Blew me straight out of the pub," said our heaviest, eighteen-stone, factory girl with peals of laughter.

Then on 7 December, without warning, we heard over the airwaves that Japan had attacked the American Pacific Fleet lying anchored in Pearl Harbour, with a devastating loss of ships and men in a matter of two hours. Simultaneously, on the western side of the International Date Line, the Japanese had bombed Hong Kong and Malaysia, and the Japanese Army had landed in southern Thailand and northern Malaysia. On that same fateful day they had also launched an attack on the American air base at Clark Field in the Philippines.

All at once the *World* was at War.

"7 December," said Roosevelt, "is the date which will go down in infamy". America had instantly declared War on Japan and Hitler had declared War on the United States. Suddenly, America was at war in two oceans.

And with frightening speed, on Christmas Day, the Japanese had captured Hong Kong; on 8 February, 1942, Rangoon the capital of Burma, fell to the Japanese; and on 15 February the Japanese had captured Singapore. By 19 February they were bombing Darwin in Australia, and on 9 April, Ceylon. Fatefully, on 6 May, they captured the Philippines.

But the fall of Singapore had been Churchill's 'Waterloo'. Singapore had been a fortress armed with 15-inch guns and 20,000 men. While Singapore's defences were looking out to sea, the Japanese were quietly using bicycles and walking through the jungle on the landward side and inflicted a humiliating defeat on the British who had thought the jungle was impenetrable.

For the next two years, the pressure on the flax industry to supply the armed forces with essential fibres escalated. At Howden,

HM Yorkshire East Riding (Howden) Flax Factory: 1939–45.

Flax straw from retting tanks spread out to dry in open air.

the machines were silent only once, to allow the shift on duty to listen to Churchill's famous "...sweat, toil, and tears" call to the nation to fight to the last man. Then came a day of great jubilation for our Italian prisoners-of-war. On 8 September, 1943, the Italians announced their surrender. The Germans moved to occupy Rome and on 13 October Italy declared War on Germany. That Christmas marked a turning point and inspired a message from Lord De La Warr to all the country's flax factory managers. To Howden he wrote: "All best wishes for a good Christmas. Certainly none deserves a better. It has been a great joy working this year in a show that is rapidly becoming a real team – a successful, confident team – and you yourself with your combination of hard working staying powers and unfailing cheeriness have made a very real contribution to it. All the best of good wishes for the New Year. Yours very sincerely, De La Warr."

Chapter 4

Flight

Germany's surrender on 29 April, 1945 and Hitler's suicide a day later had been celebrated with magnanimity. On 8 May, to a rapturous London street multitude, Churchill had given the VE sign, his hand raised high in a gesture of triumph. But the struggle for the Pacific was far from over. Fighting the Japanese in the jungles of Burma had been bitter, hazardous and awful, one of the nastiest engagements of the whole war. It had taken until 3 September, 1945, before the Japanese unconditional surrender to the Americans in Tokyo Bay aboard USS *Missouri*, and until 13 September in Burma to the Allies. At that point, I decided to call it a day, after six long years of compulsory War work in a reserved occupation.

My cousin Dennis had been taken prisoner in the first wave of Japanese attacks. Cousin Colin, a bomber pilot, had been shot down over Paris on D Day and cousin Betty had been blown up in a German air raid over London. My mother had not survived the war. My father had remarried. Our home had been sold up and my surviving sister was nursing wounded soldiers at St Thomas's Hospital in London.

My resignation from the Howden Flax Factory so soon after the end of the War was not well received. Letters of protest poured in; but I was completely exhausted. I had been assured by Home Flax Production, my factory would continue in operation – to the huge relief of anxious factory workers.

I left for London to stay with a cousin. And I slept, and slept, and slept!

Chapter 5

Bill, Elsie and I

Released by the Ministry of Supply from the constraint of wartime 'reserved occupation' and its enduring pressures, I had been approached by the Colonial Office to join a pioneer venture in Gambia, West Africa, one of Britain's oldest and smallest colonies. All along the West African coast her infamous reputation, 'white man's grave', was still common parlance, sudden death rising out of her swamps in one plague after another – malaria, blackwater, yellow fever, sleeping sickness, dysentery. Yet on 3 May, 1947, I boarded a converted Dakota aircraft for an exciting new life. Watching from behind a high wire airport fence was my mother's sister, Kate. "Whatever does she want to go to Africa for?" she had asked herself as she saw the plane soar away.

Elsie, who had also been 'hunted' for this venture, had left England earlier by ship with all our gear – camp beds, mosquito nets, tables, chairs, tin plates, cutlery, water bottles, hurricane lamps, a medicine chest and much besides. Bill, leader of the enterprise, had gone ahead to get mud huts built in an up-country village where we were to spend the next three years; and on 4 May we had planned to get together at the BOAC rest house in Bathurst (modern Banjul). Instead, I was languishing in Bordeaux in a seedy hotel bare of luxuries in the aftermath of war. It had been our first stopover. The pilot had overshot the runway and hit a pile of steel mats. The aircraft nose-dived into the ground. Miraculously, the undercarriage tearing through the plane's belly had missed the fuel tank by a hair's-breadth, saving our lives. A French woman waiting for another flight had become hysterical and gone home as fire engines and ambulances roared up, surrounding the aircraft. And here we were, eleven shocked passengers on a cold wet morning, waiting for a relief plane. It was Labour Day in France. Everybody was out marching on the streets.

But our ordeal was far from over as we set off again. We hit a storm over the Bay of Biscay. Shrouded in blankets we were still chilled to the bone as our converted aircraft soared above 12,000 ft to escape its fury.

Then there was another night's stopover in Portugal; and on again to descend in the North African desert for refuelling. Eight tribesmen, in colourful garments and feathered headdress, lined alongside the plane as it touched down. There was no visible runway, simply unending desert under a baking sun. In the distance, a wooden hut housed a latrine in curious isolation. The plane was refuelled by hand pump. And so after three days we finally reached Bathurst. In a thundering descent we clattered to a halt on a wartime runway, constructed from metal sheeting.

We were to dine at Government House that evening and made a dash in an open truck from the BOAC rest house where we were billeted, dust-covered and wild about the head, to be welcomed by the Governor, Sir Andrew Wright, who did not bat an eyelid at the sight of us.

Having presented our credentials, we set off next day for the interior in a Bedford lorry following the south bank of the Gambia River for almost a hundred miles. Travelling with us we had six Africans armed with axes and cutlasses. There were no roads up-country and we were dependent on tribal footpaths where obstructing bush and trees had to be cleared before we could continue our journey. About halfway, we had to cross a tributary of the river on a cumbersome, slow-moving contraption pulled by a steel hand rope. Below, crocodiles muddied the water.

At last we reached the village where we were to spend the next three years – surprised by a huge baboon, 'sentinel at the gate'. But that was not our only welcome. At the sight of Elsie and I with our white faces, the village women fled into the bush.

But an incident which occurred shortly after our arrival happily sealed their acceptance of our presence. We were relaxing on the mosquito-netted extension to Bill's hut drinking 'warm' beer, catching the last of the daylight before darkness fell like a blind pulled over a window, when we were horrified to see a snake crawl from Elsie's thatched roof opposite. Bill grabbed his gun and shot it. The snake dropped to the ground with a plop. Satisfied that the reptile was dead, Bill stretched it out. "Seventeen feet," he exclaimed. "It's a Green Mamba, one of the deadliest snakes in Africa. Kills in seconds."

By now, villagers had gathered and were chattering excitedly. A muscular-looking man of exceptional height stepped forward and wound the snake round his body. And off they went with this prized trophy.

It proved to be our passport to acceptance into the community;

each was given an African name which had subtle meanings lost to us. Imperceptibly, we were being drawn into the consuming web of their primordial society.

Gambia had claimed a hero of her own, the eighteenth century explorer Mungo Park who had chosen the Gambia route when setting out to discover the course of the River Niger. As a young doctor, not yet twenty-four years of age, Park had offered his services to the England-based African Association and was accepted as a geographical missionary with instructions to gather information on the rise, the course and the termination of the Niger; and on the various towns that inhabit its borders. In May, 1795, impatient and alone, he left England aboard the brig *Endeavour* – a trading ship bound for Gambia to load up with beeswax and ivory – a voyage which took thirty days to reach Gambia. Likewise, as we ourselves found one hundred and fifty years on, the rains fell in June, sealing off one village from another with dense forest and bush. Likewise, Park, too, was shut in from the world outside till the onset of the dry season in December when he was able to continue his journey. "I had parted from the last Europeans I might probably behold," Park reflected, "perhaps quitted forever the comforts of Christian society." During August he had gone down with fever but he had used his time to learn phonetic Mandinke and the native customs from a friendly Mandingo named Johnson.

Setting off again, he had not gone far when he was stopped by a native who said he must pay duty to the King in Walli; this was to become, he said, the most familiar aspect of his African travel – a custom which stayed with us known as '*a dash*!'. As the intrepid Scot moved east he found a mixture of Islam and paganism, blacks who together with the ceremonial part of the Mohammedan religion retained all their ancient superstitions – as also did we a hundred and fifty years later. Robbed and temporarily held captive by savage Moorish horsemen, worn down by sickness, hunger and exhaustion, empty-pocketed and in despair, Park soon discovered that "within a few miles, conditions could vary from spear-waving hostility to open-handed hospitality". And he had had the good fortune to meet up with a group of friendly refugees heading east. Two weeks later, on 20 July, 1796, a year after he had left England, Mungo Park saw the Niger – "with infinite pleasure the great object of my mission, the long-sought-for majestic Niger glittering in the morning sun".

Several months later he was back in Gambia, wasted by illness, to hear surprised villagers say they believed he had been killed by Moors. He joined as ship's surgeon on an American slaver, the *Charlestown,* bound for Carolina loaded with 130 slaves. It was a leaky vessel which after thirty-five days at sea had to dock in Antigua. Eleven slaves had died on the journey.

Park changed to the *Chesterfield* mail boat and arrived in England on 22 December, 1797. But he could not settle. Two years of married life and country doctoring in Peebles made him long to be on the move again; and four years later he started on his second journey to the Niger, this time taking with him a garrison of soldiers who had volunteered to accompany him. Once again, he had arrived in Gambia at the beginning of the rains. His men fell sick with dysentery and vomiting, and by the time he had reached the Niger three-quarters had died; and all his pack animals had died or been stolen. The lethal effects of the West African climate during the rains had taken their toll. But Park, exhausted and half-crazed, wrote: "I once more saw the Niger rolling its immense stream along the plain."

On 20 November, 1805, Park and his pathetic band of soldiers embarked on the schooner *Joliba*, pushed off from the Sansanding shore and disappeared "into the troubled waters of historical conjecture". Not another word was heard from him.

But the storytellers had kept his memory alive and we listened to their tales in the dark evenings around a log fire – ourselves closed in for a long stay with the onset of the June 1947 rains so soon after we had arrived.

The phonetic spelling of our village was 'Jenyr', a cluster of mud and thatch huts in Lower River Division on the south bank. It was a remote spot and to make our presence known to Tony Baldock, the District Commissioner, we had to row across the mighty river to his colonial residence at Kerewan on the north bank – a hazardous journey in a hollowed out tree trunk. Tony was a short, wiry, spirited man who accepted our credentials with a wry humour – and took more delight in showing us his magnificent cashew-nut tree. And so we rowed the tedious crossing back to become the 'permanent guests' of the district's hereditary chief, Landing Sanneh – an autocratic Mandingo of advancing years whose 'palatial kingdom' was only a bush path away in the next village. There he would sit in his deckchair in prominent view with his ancient hammer-bell alarm clock on the ground beside him. No one dared ignore his summons at the shrill sound of the alarm bell.

And the next village to Kaiaf, the chief's seat, was Toniataba. Beyond was an ironstone escarpment and rock.

We listened through an interpreter to the story of Jenyr.

A Mandingo hunter from Guinea, Mamba Sanneh, while wandering through the forest with his followers, had come across a stream and had exclaimed "*jay nyeolu*" ("there fishes"); and they had built a village near the stream (bolon) winding its way into the River Gambia. But they were invaded by fanatical Mohammedans from the north bank of the river – a family named Jarju and their followers. From that time, local wars and slave-raids raged continuously between the pagans and the Moslems.

Suddenly, one extremely old villager began muttering about a man he called Fodi Kabba who had pillaged and terrorised for years; till the white men's boats came up the river. The old man had raised his voice to a crescendo to describe a "very big battle" at Toniataba. Fodi Kabba was defeated. His power had been broken. And he had gone into hiding – only to be blown up when a powder magazine exploded during a bombardment.

Bill had asked the meaning of *Fodi*?

"It means *Defender of the Faith*," said our interpreter.

I was passing one of the mud and thatch huts when a large middle-aged woman in colourful dress and headdress came rushing out and pushed forward a youth.

"Take him," she cried.

She was not from the village, I thought probably an itinerant trader. I stopped and turned to the young man. We looked long at each other without uttering a word. For something had happened, a mystical feeling of natural bonding, of two kindred spirits.

"His name is Ebou," the woman broke the illusory moment.

Bill had taken on a Mauritanian, a pale-faced charming rogue with a little knowledge of medicine. Elsie was in the huts noting what the women were cooking. At four o'clock each morning we could hear the thump, thump, of pestle and mortar as they pounded. Ebou and I followed the men, their axes over their shoulders, who walked single file into the forest to 'slash-and-burn' an area ready to plant. And in the long dark evenings of the rainy season we gathered together over a log fire and listened engrossed to the Mauritanian's tales of wars between the invading Muslims from the north and the pagan territorial kings of Gambia – wars, he said, which had been carried across the river close to Jenyr when surrounding villages had been burnt down. "Many people fled to the coast," he said.

Ebou and I had gathered a team of six Jenyr men to record the 'slash-and burn' system of growing food. None could speak English but all could write in basic Arabic which Ebou could translate. It had been their choice of a leader which had surprised. His name was Jarju. Ebou said he was a descendant of the family of Jarju from the north bank and we became keenly interested in the social hierarchy of the village community – the Sannehs, who were descendants of the founder-settlers and held every important position in the village; the Jarjus, immigrants who though close to the Sannehs were still classed as strangers; and households whose occupants were descended from slaves taken in local wars.

The Mauritanian had kept us amused with his fables and tales of local wars and, reminiscent of Mungo Park, in the light of a lamp seated on a mat on the ground, we too heard the women sing.

The wind roared and the rain fell.
The poor white man faint and weary
Come and sat under our tree…
Let us pity the poor white man.

CHAPTER 6

CROCODILE CREEK

B ut we were beginning to wilt in the thrashing storm rains, the exhausting humidity, the relentless tropical sun. Bill had been seized by an itch to change things. Several hundred miles east in Tanganyika, bulldozers were tearing down vast wildernesses of tangled bush. In military style, an inspired scheme to grow groundnuts and "win against every obstacle a prize of food for the hungry of the world" had just hit the headlines. Bill wanted to fell the forest on our doorstep and create a 'garden of Eden' forest behind the village which had been merely scratched for food and firewood for centuries by men with primitive axes, the undisturbed haunts of lions, baboons, wild pig. Bill began striding the village like a man possessed. I agreed to make a trip to Bathurst and find out if land-clearing equipment was available. There was none; and I took the governor's launch back which would call at Yellitenda close by Jenyr. Post-war 1947 and Bathurst had yet to awaken from its sleepy pre-war existence.

But disaster struck. Shortly before reaching Jenyr waters, the launch broke down. Desperate, the captain spotted a lone dugout and vigorously hailed the fisherman. Turning to the only white man among us, he said: "Jump in and he'll take you up the Jenyr creek to get help from the doctor there."

He was an Irishman, tall, sunburnt with thick wavy hair. He had flatly refused. It would soon be dark. Frustrated, his launch filled with native passengers travelling further up-country, the captain turned to me: "You are from Jenyr. Will you go?"

I climbed into the dugout, helped by my personal servant Brima who had been travelling with me. Then he climbed in, a hefty fellow, to the consternation of the fisherman as his boat dipped and rocked. Slowly, with his single paddle, the fisherman rowed us toward the mouth of the bolon (creek) when the dugout got stuck in the mud. The two men got out and struggled to push the boat clear. And I got out to help. "Get back in," they cried. "Plenty crocodiles see white legs!" Minutes later they had the dugout clear and cautiously we entered the creek. It was pitch black by now.

"You have torch light?" said Brima. It was the one piece of equipment I never travelled without.

Very slowly the fisherman rowed up the long, winding creek, making no sound with his paddle, while Brima flashed the torch along the bank sides looking for lurking crocodiles. And every so often they would whisper: "bamba! bamba!"

To his utter amazement, Bill saw the flickering torch light as we walked into the village just as Brima let out a terrible scream. He had trodden on a scorpion. My bag, which he had been head-loading, flew to the ground. Mercifully, Bill was right there with his expert medical skills.

In the heat of the moment we had forgotten the governor's launch perilously afloat in the middle of the Gambia. Bill wrote a note to the Yellitenda crossing ferry master and called one of the Jenyr boys. He wedged the note into a stick, gave the stick to the boy and told him to run the ten miles or so to Yellitenda and safely deliver the note.

Bill had said to me: "There's no alternative. You'll have to make a trip to England to purchase a bulldozer and agricultural machinery." But I had delayed the visit until the men and women in the village had gathered in their harvest from the 1947 plantings. I would not sacrifice completion of my 1947 records of 'slash-and-burn' and hand hoe methods of feeding the family through Bill's haste to bring in big machines.

And so it was shortly after Christmas that I left for England. Three weeks later, I returned to Gambia with all Bill's requests satisfactorily in place. I could not have foreseen what I found on reaching Jenyr. Bill and Elsie had flown!

Chapter 7

Rumours at King Rock

I was alone!

Bill's and Elsie's mud and thatch huts stood locked up and empty. My hurricane lamp shone like a beacon as darkness fell. Figures moved silently across my mosquito-netted window casting eerie shadows.

Bill had gone. I had come.

Had Bill been too long in Africa? And what shall we do with the bulldozer Bill had set his heart on? It had arrived, travelled from Bathurst under its own power in the hands of an expert African driver, clearing a ninety-mile swathe of forest bush in its path.

Gambia, the oldest British colony in West Africa, always neglected by Britain, had suffered many killing diseases. In 1869, Bathurst, the capital, had lost 1,000 of its 4,000 population to the great cholera outbreak. At this latter day, in 1947, the Human Nutrition Research Unit of the Colonial Medical Research Council had set up laboratories, with the aid of post-Second World War Colonial Development and Welfare Funds, for the study of diseases of Gambia; and had begun its researches in and around the coastal zone of Fajara (close by Bathurst) and the up-river field station at Keneba in Western Kiang District on the south bank, Gambia River (about twenty miles west of Jenyr).

We in Jenyr had arrived in Gambia several months earlier. It had been envisaged that over the next three years we would have gained a thorough understanding of the food systems, social attitudes and life-styles of a rural community in the heart of Africa.

Jenyr villagers had simply reverted to their centuries-old way of life as if we had never been. But land clearing and farm machinery for which Bill had asked began arriving in unstoppable waves.

We were still in the long dry season, a parching Harmattan wind scorching the upland sandy soils. The men were out in the forest a good two miles from the village with their axes cutting down trees and burning debris. The women were down in the swamp transplanting rice seedlings. And no one saw two mischievous boys get hold of a recently-delivered hand winch. They wound the steel cable round the massive girth of an ancient tree and, laughing and joking, pulled on the handle. The tree would not budge. They tried again, and again, and again, laughing and shouting, when suddenly the steel rope snapped, caught the rays of the sun as the jagged edges flew into the air and whipped back to lacerate the leg of one of the boys and the arm of the other.

All at once, a menacing crowd had gathered calling for the witch doctor!

"We must take them as quickly as possible to the Victoria Hospital," I said, anxious that somehow we had to make the ninety miles to Bathurst.

"You'um cut off limbs," they cried. "Witch doctor come. He no cut off limbs. Must die with whole body."

To break the deadlock, I promised not to let the hospital doctor cut off either the arm or the leg, got the boys on to our Bedford lorry, and agreed to take a number of the villagers who had climbed in. We set off under a searing midday sun for the long slow journey on a bumpy, dust-laden dirt track.

It had just struck midnight as we reached the Victoria Hospital. The door was closed and I rang the bell and knocked loudly. At last a Gambian porter opened it and took one look at the boys.

"Only Africans," he said and pushed the door shut; but I had my foot in it.

"Please fetch the doctor *now*," I said.

"He sleeping."

"You'um wake him." We had the boys lifted into the hall. Within the hour, a young doctor of about thirty-five appeared, dressed in tweeds, shaved and smiling. He had the boys taken to his surgery. I followed to hear his assessment of the wounds.

"I can repair the leg," he said. "I shall have to amputate the arm."

"You cannot amputate," I said. "It is against their beliefs."

"And if the boy dies?"

"We'll have to go ahead on a prayer."

He hesitated, and it was an anxious moment. "Very well," he said to my relief, and began the long night through with infinite care as I watched him operate.

Late the next morning I visited the boys in their hospital beds. No amputation had taken place. The boys, tucked between clean sheets, were surrounded by their kinsmen who had travelled with us. And everyone was smiling and nodding and exclaiming "*Yo! Yo!*" which may be translated "Very good, Very good".

In Jenyr a drama of its own was unfolding.

Nearby Toniataba was again in the forefront of Gambia River's sad and turbulent history blemished by its share in supplying slaves to the New World. It was less than sixty years, in 1892, since Fodi Kabba, a robber chief who had been terrorizing the neighbourhood with bloodthirsty ferocity, was finally defeated in a ferocious battle at Toniataba by white men coming up the river in boats. Old men in Jenyr were enthralling us with tales of that last ferocious battle which finally broke the power of Fodi Kabba.

Today, as we returned from Bathurst, it was the destructive Harmattan wind that had delivered a mortal blow to the villagers of Toniataba.

A poor old woman had accidentally spilt oil from her cooking pot on to the fire. Instantly, the vicious wind had whipped up the flames which spread like lightning to destroy every homestead in the village.

It was a sight to behold as the villagers of Jenyr snaked in single file along bush tracks, each head-loading gifts of food for their distraught kinsmen huddled among the ashes of their burnt-out village.

The rains had come early to clear the air from the exhausting heat and promised to be unusually heavy this year. Naked Jenyr children were jumping and splashing in the puddles and the whole village had suddenly come alive.

On our journey back from the Victoria Hospital, we had not escaped passing through a massive dust bowl created by an army of bulldozers which had ripped up a vast area of trees in the coastal region – bulldozers in such number that it had been possible for Bill to have one sent up to Jenyr, a 'white elephant' which was still blocking the entrance to the village.

Another post-war Britain adventure had sprung up like magic.

We had heard that a team of experts were setting up the world's largest poultry farm with the aim of supplying Britain's breakfast tables with twenty million eggs a year. And as our vehicle slithered and swerved in the dust, we had come across a couple of gloomy-looking white men and we asked them about the miles of chicken runs.

"Rhode Island Reds are being flown in," they said.

"How are you going to feed such a large flock of birds?"

"Pigeon peas," one said, "but even the pigeon pea will find it difficult to grow in all this dust."

"You wait and see," the other added disdainfully. "Rhode Island Reds are tough birds. They'll survive."

All along the three hundred miles of Gambia, five miles north and five miles south of the river to the borders with north and south French Senegal, villagers, hidden behind forest and tall grasses, oblivious of the bustling coastline, were hacking out tiny plots and dropping seeds into holes in the ground with great speed now that the rains had come in full flood.

But the people of Jenyr had not been so keen to leave the village when they heard a rumour that a lion was prowling. They sent the lookout man up a palm tree; but for three whole days he saw nothing. Then suddenly he cried: "Over there!" And a shot rang out. Everyone hurried to the spot. There they found the young mechanic Bill had hired, still around, holding the gun Bill had given him when he left, staring in amazement at the lion he had just killed.

Only it was a lioness he had killed, a most beautiful creature laid out before us.

Ebou's team were relentlessly following the villagers as they hoed and weeded and recording the time they spent working and resting; while flash floods in the torrential rains eroded the fine upland sandy soils and lightning streaked across the sky with crashing rolls of thunder. Jenyr was closed to the villages around by the ferocious growth of tall grasses and forest regeneration.

But for Chief Landing Sanneh in his 'kingdom of Kaiaf', and for his people of Jenyr and the surrounding villages, a decision by our colonial masters to re-site the District Commissioner's headquarters from Kerewan, on the north bank, to a site on the south bank of the river was exciting speculation. In late November as the 1948 harvest was being gathered, expatriates from Bathurst started building at a place on the deserted rocky ironstone escarpment east of Toniataba; and they named the new district headquarters *Mansa Konko*, 'King rock'.

Chapter 8

Goodbye to Jenyr

It was sad that Tony, our District Commissioner, did not live to make the transfer from Kerewan to his new headquarters at Mansa Konko. While on a visit to Sierra Leone, his jeep had skidded off a highland track and plunged into a ravine, killing both himself and his African driver. Shortly after, Jack, his replacement, arrived to take up residence at Mansa Konko.

Suddenly, Chief Landing Sanneh's fief buzzed with new arrivals. Jack had brought his wife and infant little girl with him. An agricultural advisor from South Africa was appointed to the district, who also came with his wife and infant son. And Jenyr, after months of isolation following Bill's departure, had become the focus of attention for the mandarins of the Medical Research Council's new tropical research establishment at Fajara near Bathurst.

And I now had a jeep at my disposal. I made the seven or so miles, crossing a major causeway, through Toniataba to Mansa Konko, to meet our new Commissioner for the first time. The river, swollen during the heavy rains, lapped ominously against the sides of the causeway which was just wide enough to take the jeep.

Jack, in his late thirties, was tall with an easy manner and an engaging smile. We lunched together and, having established our presence in his District, I headed back to Jenyr. I was just about halfway across the causeway when the ugly head of a crocodile emerged from the left bank right in front of the jeep. I pulled up sharply as his huge body spread across the causeway in front of the bonnet. And there he rested. There had been a rumour that a man-eating crocodile had slipped behind the mangrove but I had thought nothing of it. Petrified, I clutched the steering wheel. What was the hideous reptile thinking as he stayed motionless with his head over the right side and his tail over the left side of the causeway? The jeep's engine was still running. Would the smell of petrol send him off? Time stood still. I was terrified that with one sweep of his tail this powerful reptile would crash the jeep and leave me for dead.

Suddenly, he pulled his incredibly large body forward. His tail swept across the causeway. And the man-eating crocodile plunged with a big splash back into the swirling waters.

Brenda, a newly qualified nutritionist, had arrived to replace Elsie – a bubbling, hefty young girl full of excitement at her first experience of Africa. And then there was John. He came with his wife and baby girl. Now we were three adults again for the final year of recording life in a rural African village.

But we had agricultural machinery from Bill's earlier venture which could not be allowed to remain unused; and four fifty-acre experimental plots of varying soil types around the village were marked out. One plot on the edge of the village had been selected for its virgin forest cover. Here, Ebou and I with survey equipment, and two or three villagers with axes, emerged from the dense forest canopy. We had cleared a trace for a rectangular plot; and with our standard Fordson tractor with blade, supported by considerable manpower, a stupendous effort went ahead to clear fifty acres of virgin forest.

The overlay of costly, at times inappropriate experiments, the sudden comings and goings of expatriates from the coast with meddlesome ideas of their own which they wished to promote, had to be contained to safeguard uninterrupted ongoing recordings of the villagers' life-styles for the third and final year, for which we at Jenyr had originally been appointed by our colonial masters.

And so the three European residents at Jenyr were calling it a day in late November 1949, having declined offers to renew contracts for a further period. For myself, I had but one thought. The three-year survey results must be written up or be lost; and time, and the right environment, were needed for the task.

With much heart-searching, we said goodbye to Jenyr, and took to the road for Bathurst and our onward flights. Once again, our rough track to Bathurst took us through the £1 million poultry adventure only to find it in total disarray and closing down. The Rhode Island Reds had not flourished. It had been impossible to feed the feathered army and the exceptional rainy season had killed off most of the birds.

Meanwhile, the skinny little native-owned Gambian fowls were producing eggs the size of marbles, as they had done for centuries. And thousands of native farmers were still using the hand-hoe as their only tool. But two important pieces of legislation were about to make their impact: 'bush fires' were to be banned and sixpence was to be given for every monkey's tail presented.

PART TWO

CHAPTER 9

MILLIONAIRES' AVENUE

The world was hungry!

We had returned from Africa to a post-War Britain which was acutely short of fats and oils. The recommendation of 'three wise men' had been taken that only by using mechanised equipment on vast tracts of unoccupied land to produce oil-rich groundnuts could the shortfall be met. The red plain in Tanganyika (later renamed Tanzania) had seemed ideal.

In 1947, men had been sent out in great haste to clear scrubby bush, with caterpillar tractors and blades, in this deserted wasteland – and plant groundnuts. A military-style encampment had sprung up which shone by night in a blaze of light surrounded by mile upon mile of uninhabited darkness; elephants wandered in search of water, hyenas came noisily close. Five years later, the debacle of this vast East African Groundnut Scheme was about to hit the headlines.

At home, men and women in their late twenties and thirties, back from the War, were competing with fresh-faced school-leavers for university places. My write-up of our three years in Jenyr finally in the press, I too became a late entrant. I had become a student again. I had been admitted to St Hilda's College at Oxford University.

But the day I received my degree, I was on a flight back to Africa. I had been sent to assess what could be salvaged from Tanganyika's failed groundnut scheme. The 'three wise men' had overlooked that there was not sufficient rainfall on that red plain.

The long flight to Dar-es-Salaam was only the beginning. I was on my way to Nachingwea, headquarters of the Tanganyika Groundnut Scheme.

I had boarded a train, fired on wood and capable of no more than twenty miles an hour, for Tabora to join a staff member with a station wagon for the last lap of the journey. This took us south, crossing a vast empty sandy plain, clouds of dust rising blown by the winds, filling our eyes, noses and throats.

I had left England in the summer of 1954 but the momentous three million-acre mechanised groundnut scheme had been pronounced a failure as early as July, 1949, after only two years of fleets of bulldozers bashing down bush, pushing aside all obstacles. I had been sent to enquire whether anything could be salvaged.

My first impression of Nachingwea was the high point of Millionaires' Avenue. A row of mansions built in stone with grand fire-place living rooms to house top level expatriates, stood empty in scary wind-swept isolation – except for one at the end of the street which was being used as a slaughter-house.

On the main campus, a skeleton staff had been left behind as watchdogs. They played tennis and lazed in the sun. I had been given a house which also had stood empty for some time. It was sparsely furnished with a bed, table and chair, and a kitchen with a large fridge. The kitchen was infested with big cockroaches which made a terrible noise as they scampered into the woodwork whenever I 'ran the gauntlet' to reach the fridge. The windows around the house were heavily netted with metal to keep out prowling wild animals at night; and the whole place was dark, gloomy and depressing.

I had the use of a jeep and driver, and early on paid a courtesy visit to the District Commissioner. The journey took us two or three hours through deserted woodland and rocky outcrops. But it was on the return journey that I had my first taste of the unpredictable habits of my African driver.

Suddenly, he stopped the jeep, jumped out and disappeared into the woods along the track. It was nerve-wracking. He had taken the ignition key, leaving me stranded like a sitting duck. To my right, trees, a dreadful gangrene from their roots to their ten-feet-high tops, were like a petrified forest from ghastly Grimm's fairy tales. An hour passed, and another, in this awful spot with not a soul in sight. And when he did show up, a mattress swaying awkwardly on his head, he said nothing.

No less traumatic, on another journey once again he suddenly stopped the jeep; but this time he did not get out. What he did was to turn his head to the right. Following his gaze I saw a pride of lions not ten feet away – the male a huge and beautiful creature with an extremely long mane, the lioness leaning against him, three cubs nestled between them. He had become rigid. What were we to do? When, on a prayer, I spotted a small dim light far in the distance, I suggested we make a dash for it but he would not move. In a blind panic, I got out and ran for my life towards the light. It was a gamekeeper's hut and mercifully the gamekeeper was inside. I never knew how he dealt with my driver. He had picked up his gun and gone off to sort him out.

It was Christmas Day.

They played tennis, the expatriates. The officer-in-charge of the watchdogs was a big man, strong and a keen tennis player. The skeleton African staff had taken cover from the intense heat and wind-blown dust which carried deadly microbes, and were sleeping. I had not left my house all day, was nursing a throat infection.

The folly of it, tennis in that scorching desert heat where no rain fell. I had returned to England shortly after that Christmas and declined a further contract. And it was two years later when I was participating at a Congress in Oxford that I heard my name called out. I turned. Seated against the wall was the 'big strong man' from Nachingwea; only he was shockingly wizened, shrivelled, dwarfed and dried up. His eyes shone from his mask-like face with a kind of joy at seeing someone he knew. And we chatted, pretended he was still his old self. It was a sad brief encounter.

In those two years since I left Nachingwea, I had been engaged in a home-based research project at Cambridge University and, as we talked, I felt glad I had decided that long-ago Christmas not to go back to Nachingwea with all the health risks attached.

If there had been a lesson to be learned for Africa, was it perhaps to 'go slowly and with her centuries-old know-how of her own lands?' I was about to test this theory. I would soon be leaving Cambridge, returning to Oxford, the centre of commonwealth studies, to engage in new research. Africa was calling me back.

CHAPTER 10

TRAVELLING OFF-BEAT IN INDIA

In 1959 while researching, with a grant from the Leverhulme Trust, the transition from subsistence to cash economies in Africa, I was appointed to a lectureship in tropical economics at Oxford University. I had not so far travelled in Asia, an omission which I felt I had to rectify as soon as possible; and it was in 1961, after exhaustive planning, that I took a sabbatical for an extensive tour of the Indian sub-continent, from Delhi to Bangalore, south to Madras, east to Calcutta – once again with a grant from the Leverhulme Trust.

On 15 August, 1947, India, in the words of Jawaharlal Nehru, India's first prime minister, "woke to life and freedom". In 1946, there had been the Hindu-Muslim massacres. The next year, India was independent but partitioned. Five hundred thousand people had died in the violence that had accompanied partition. And the end of empire had been sealed for Britain forever. These were propitious times.

Fourteen years had passed since Nehru's famous words. I had stepped off the plane in New Delhi, the only white passenger, and tagged along at the end of a long line of Indian arrivals to be discovered with astonishment and mild disapproval by the airport gurus. But I held a Letter of Credit and confirmation of a hotel booking at the *Janpath*, one of Delhi's best-known hotels.

At the *Janpath,* I was given a large upper room in which I both slept and ate so that Hindu guests were not disturbed by my presence. One wall of the room was mosquito-netted in place of windows which was slightly alarming when, in the middle of the night, I was woken by a hungry-looking man outside the netted window: "You like banana?" he said.

Next morning, Mahmud Ahmed turned up in his tiny Austin Seven to be my escort while I remained in Delhi – an employee of the Indian Leaf Tobacco Company who had generously offered help with transport during my travels.

Mahmud, coming up to forty years of age, had a quiet unassuming manner which belied his attractive slight figure and handsome features. We squeezed into his car and made for old Delhi and as he zigzagged through the seething street crowds, he told his story. "My father," he said, "fled with all the family from the massacres at partition to the new Muslim state of Pakistan. His house had been burnt down during the riots and he had lost everything. But I wanted to stay on. I did not want to be uprooted from the India I loved. But now the Hindus have stepped up their harassment of us Muslims who are still around."

I sensed a man haunted by indecision, fearing a new wave of terror and bloodshed, yet reluctant to pack up and go; when suddenly, rising high above the milling crowds, Mahmud pointed excitedly, calling out "*jama masquid*". We left the car and struggled in the suffocating heat up a rocky height to reach the entrance to the great mosque. Mahmud had dated the mosque from 1650 in the time of the Mogul Empire. We had removed our shoes on entering and were passing through a magnificent courtyard of granite paving inlaid with marble. Suddenly the heavens opened and torrential rain fell. But Mahmud wore an ecstatic expression of wonder and joy, which lifted him in that moment from his agitated daily round.

With Mahmud as my escort in Delhi, I had had no rounded impression of the city except perhaps for old Delhi's shouts of petty traders above the jostling crowds, and the wanderings of emaciated cows sacred to the Hindus.

I left Delhi for the villages, first by train with a stopover at Anand for a visit to a much heralded cooperative milk collecting centre which had been set up to enable poor families in the surrounding area with only a cow or two to sell the milk. I was sick, and grateful when the train stopped in Rajasthan where, under the glowering stares of large, turbaned Hindus, I made for the rest room.

Mahmud had spoken of the many gods of Hindu worship, dating back, he had said, more than two thousand centuries. "It is from Brahma that Hindu cosmology takes its structure," he had said. "Brahma is described in early myths as a universal and creative spirit, born from a golden egg and then to have created the Earth. Priestly Brahmins are seen to be coming from the mouth of Brahma," he had said, as he tried to explain caste in Hindu mythology. "Warriors come from Brahma's arms, traders from Brahma's thighs and agriculturalists from Brahma's feet. Beyond the pale in Hindu society are the untouchables, outcasts who are left with jobs regarded as impure," he had concluded. In a sense, I was myself feeling outcast right then, isolated by my fellow passengers, muscular disdainful men ignoring my existence.

I was still not well when the train reached Anand. My host from the cooperative had come to meet me and, climbing into his jeep, we bumped along rough open country assailed by wild flying peacocks overhead with their blood-curdling screams.

His home was simple, two-storied, and we climbed a wooden ladder to the upper floor where his wife had prepared an assortment of Indian dishes. To her dismay, I could not do justice to her wonderful spread; but happily, she provided a local herb which was amazingly effective in getting rid of the wretched bug which I had carried from Delhi.

We had been confined in a shed at the airport for some hours, twelve angry passengers waiting for a flight to Bombay. My host at the Anand cooperative had driven me at dawn to the small grass airport, a 'scary mile', missing cows roaming across our path with several alarming crashings of brakes; and he had gone home unaware of our predicament. The pilot was holding his ground. The passengers for the flight were pressing him to take off but he insisted there was a fault. He had sent for a relief aircraft; and he had been proved right. The aircraft would have crashed on take-off, killing all of us.

But I had occupied the long wait engrossed in a work on Indian history – the rise and fall of the Mughal Empire, their power struggles with the Rajputs in Delhi, which lasted from the twelfth century well into the eighteenth century; the relatively short period of British rule and the infamous Indian Mutiny of 1857. But Hinduism, the Hindu worship of many deities, dated back hundreds of years before Christ. It would, I pondered, take a very long period of study to understand the complexity and depth of Hinduism and its overriding influence through time.

When eventually a relief plane arrived, we reached Bombay without further incident to find a seething cosmopolitan city in turmoil; after fourteen years of independence, the city was still uncertain of its place in the restructuring of the new India.

But I was on my way south to Bangalore and had only stayed overnight in this bustling, energetic, crowded city.

There was a surprising sense of Englishness in Bangalore and a somewhat relaxed atmosphere. Yet an unnatural silence hovered over this glorious 'kingdom' on the banks of the Cauvery River. I had been given a room overlooking the Cauvery in a palatial building set behind a massive colonnade; and I had been the only guest in this eerie, haunting emporium with its mile-long walk down empty corridors which had once echoed with the footsteps of local potentates.

But happily, an Indian family called next day and invited me to their home till my onward flight to Madras.

Before leaving England, I had written to a young Indian lady at Madras University who I had discovered shared a common interest. I had read the work of Gilbert Slater who in 1916, while Professor of Indian Economics at Madras, had sent his students out to the villages to "make surveys of ordinary contemporary village life with, as its central object of study, the causes of and remedies for Indian poverty". In 1918, Slater published his book *Some South Indian Villages*.

Twenty years later, a former student of Slater's had resurveyed these villages and, against a count of wants and failures, had nonetheless found the villages better linked with road and rail. I was setting out to again resurvey these villages twenty-five years on; and I was to be joined by Meenakshi who had long wished to go out into the villages. A woman travelling alone from her seat at the university had not been possible. But two women travelling together? I flew in from Bangalore. And there she was, a solitary figure waiting at the edge of the grassy strip, clutching her sari from the gusty landing.

Meenakshi had rushed us to the railway station for the night train. There had been no question of staying over in Madras before we set off to the villages, of getting to know one another first. Instead, she hustled us to the station and kept up an air of secrecy as we pushed our way into an overcrowded women's carriage and took window seats. Sitting opposite, she was rigid, staring straight over my head, saying nothing. And I wondered if she was afraid of something.

She had a slim, rather graceful, figure under her sari of fine silk, her sleek black hair neatly drawn back. The carriage was packed with women and children, children squatting under the seats, peering out like birds waiting for crumbs as the women brought curry-smelling food from greasy newspapers. Meenakshi was clutching our water container, ignoring the appealing eyes of the woman next her.

About two o'clock the train came to a halt. "We get out here," said Meenakshi, struggling to get to the door before the train moved off. There had been a few passengers alighting and they had disappeared into the night. Meenakshi pointed to a seat outside the station. Somewhat nervously she said: "They are sending someone to meet us." I had tried to find out more but she had been extremely reticent. And so we waited, watched the sun rise as dawn broke, when suddenly an ox cart came crawling up. A very thin sleepy driver and Meenakshi exchanged a few words and we climbed into the cart.

Ambling along as a hot sun rose toward midday we came at last to a village displaying a large banner as we entered which read: 'Welcome to our guests'. We had reached the Brahmin village of Dusi and we were met by a prosperous-looking landowner who took us into the village for lunch. But then came the first shock. This was, it emerged, a caste-held village; and I, a Christian, was an out-caste. From the small aperture in a round mud hut in which I had been left, I could see Meenakshi seated on the ground with a group of dignitaries before a tantalising spread of delicacies. And when they had finished a leisurely lunch, they came for me to rejoin the party on a tour of the village as though there had been nothing untoward. That night, we were to stay in Conjeeveram, seven kilometres from Dusi, a great commercial centre and a revered place of pilgrimage; and this time it was not by ox cart but by the village plutocrat's luxury transport that we travelled.

Meenakshi was enthralled by the city's temples and moved to enter one. As she disappeared into its dark recess I noticed the sign over the door. *'Entry is forbidden to Christians Muslims and dogs'*; and when Meenakshi emerged, her face shone in a kind of ecstasy. Next morning, we left this teeming city of pilgrimage for a gruelling tour of the villages, the more remote the more primitive and the more difficult to reach. Two women travelling alone, and we were locked up overnight in one village prison. In another, we had arrived to find total panic among the residents; it transpired that all the wells had dried up. We heard that only one well had water but that was in the untouchable caste quarter. The crisis among the populace was overwhelming and we left with nothing solved.

And so we journeyed on in slow trains, spending hours on uncomfortable slatted seats, sleeping locked-in on railway stations. In one village we found a woman drawing water from a polluted tank (small dam) who beckoned us into her primitive hut. She had an infant in her arms: "All my eight children have died," she said. "This one I want to keep." She wept over the baby. "Cholera," Meenakshi said. In another village, Meenakshi had been incensed at the treatment of a group of women who had been lined up in single file and were being driven into a wooden building – only to reappear minutes later screaming. "They are being sterilized," said Meenakshi. "The government has a birth control policy," she said, "but this is a cruel way of interpreting it."

By the time we had resurveyed, for the second time, villages Gilbert Slater had first targeted in 1916, we were utterly exhausted. Far in the shadow of the Western Ghats bordering Kerala, we had secured two seats on the night express train to Madras. Two men had already occupied the carriage and taken the upper bunks. "Keep your bags away from the window," they warned as pathetically thin figures stretched on the running board were thrusting their arms through the iron bars of the unglazed apertures. "As soon as the train starts they will fall to their death like flies," said one of the men. I turned to Meenakshi; but she had already fallen asleep.

"The head of my department was very upset," Meenakshi had said when we met again after we had rested from the journey. "Two women travelling alone into our villages! It is unheard of," he had chastised her. Meenakshi had laughed. "I had been worried we might be missed and someone sent out to find us."

Meenakshi and her university friend had brought a picnic where we could relax and enjoy the fresh breezes off the sea, sitting on a grassy bank far from the crowded city streets. For the next day I would be leaving Madras for lesser-known parts of Eastern India. It was a cherished 'moment of tranquility'. For out of our bold venture into the hinterland, our at times traumatic experiences, we had found a kindred spirit beyond vast differences in race and culture.

And so I left Madras (Chennai) on the Calcutta express, locked by the station master into a carriage, praying that someone would let me out when I reached my destination, Vijayawada, in South Andhra Pradesh, India's most aggressive and politically active State. Sure enough, the key was turned by another station master when the train pulled up in Vijayawada and there on the platform Stan was waiting.

Stan was a lanky Englishman married to Gena, a rather charming Anglo-Indian lady; and they were to be my hosts for the next few days. Stan was the local manager of a tobacco-drying plant, saddened that soon they would have to leave India and their beautiful home. "An Indian will be taking over," Stan said. "Neither does independent India like Anglo-Indians. We will be settling in Cornwall." Their hospitality was a welcome break before setting off on a journey across Andhra and Orissa. Stan had said: "It's dirt track and pretty rough where you're going: my driver can take you in our station wagon to the Godavari River crossing. That's about a day's drive."

I had intended to stopover in Rajamundry.

"Take the boat across the Godavari and you'll be there," Stan had said. "There's a good hostelry."

But Stan's driver had taken a route through the nearby village of Amaravati to show off statues of the Buddha. "During the monsoon," he said, "boats gather at the jetty and follow the Krishna River all the way to Vijayawada." And he pointed to lotus symbols on the feet of statues of the Buddha, the tightly curled head of hair and long earlobes, which he said were indications of an enlightened teacher. It had been a fascinating diversion and it was quite late by the time we reached the Godavari River and I had taken the boat over to Rajamundry and checked into a hostel. But within the hour a delightful local Indian family, Dr and Mrs Reddy, had called and invited me to stay with them. And it was during my visit that Mrs Reddy suggested we went to the Picture Palace.

The Picture Palace was barred to women which apparently was a constant frustration to Mrs Reddy. "It's worth a try," she had said with an air of excitement. "Taking a foreign guest." But it took a lot of wrangling and pocketfuls of rupees before we were secretly led to a dark corner of the balcony. Below, men had their eyes glued upon the screen.

"Look at them!" Mrs Reddy said scornfully. "They sit in public eating-houses and spend hours at the Picture Palace neglecting their wives and children."

"Always the same show too," Dr Reddy said later. "They never tire of it." But Mrs Reddy was not going to forget our night at the Picture Palace.

And Dr Reddy had said: "We'll get you an excellent guide for your onward journey into Orissa. You'll be perfectly safe with the guide I have in mind. He knows the area well."

We had hardly breakfasted when a large, rotund Buddha-like middle-aged man arrived seated, like some regal potentate, behind the driver in a large black car, its antiquated body resting upon a high chassis. As I climbed into the vehicle Dr Reddy whispered deferentially: "Your travel companion is a retired civil servant, a most highly respected Brahman."

Mrs Reddy rushed up and thrust a sandwich into my hand.

We had not gone far when the driver braked sharply on a bend. The tangled remains of a vehicle lay strewn over the dirt road, its occupants, all male, screaming from their wounds.

"We must call for help," I urged.

"Let them die," said my companion in a tone of authority, and he had ordered the driver to pass on.

It had worried me. Would Meenakshi have left these wretched men dying? I recalled that she had said: "In Hindu philosophy the individual human being is not the centre of the universe. The Hindu believes in reincarnation, in innumerable reincarnations without beginning, in the endless cycle of rebirths." My companion, who spoke perfect English, had simply ignored my deep concern at our offering no help.

By midday we had reached a wayside eating place and at last he broke his silence, but only to say: "You are not permitted to enter. It is forbidden to eat beef." He had referred to my sandwich but he well knew Mrs Reddy had made it strictly vegetarian. As I sat under a tree to eat my sandwich, a frail-looking man came up and squatted down beside me. He wore his dhoti, soiled with stains of red earth and the sweat of toil, loosely to the ankle and fastened between his legs. I offered to share my sandwich but he shook his head. Was he also waiting for a high-caste Brahmin to finish his meal, I wondered? We could not understand each other's language. We just stayed together under the tree. And it was a sweet moment of human warmth.

After about an hour my travel companion emerged bearing a satisfied expression and we set off again. But we had not gone far when we ran into a horrendous storm which made driving extremely hazardous.

"Will we make Rayagada before dark?" I asked anxiously. We were the only travellers on the road, which was scary.

"We are expected," said my companion with the finality of one who does not wish to be spoken to again.

Suddenly the dirt road ended. In front of us was a river raging under the storm.

"We will cross," said my companion to my utter amazement. *Where? How?* I asked myself nervously. But the driver had released the hand brake and we were slipping into the water, borne by the high chassis of the car to the middle of the river when the engine stalled. As the water lashed against the sides of the car we seemed to be facing certain death. Unperturbed, my companion stayed motionless like some ancient seer, his hands folded over his vast chest; and I turned to where he was looking. On the other bank, bullock cart drivers and several bullocks had plunged into the water. All at once the car was surrounded by floundering bullocks and men swimming alongside. Five rupees to pull us out they were demanding. "One," repeated the Brahman, unyielding, as I pleaded with him in vain to give them what they asked. A bullock's head came through the car window on my side. Terrified by our whole predicament, I pushed it back with all my strength; when suddenly the bullock drivers capitulated and a virtual army of swimmers began to push us to safety.

But the car had to be dried out before it would start up; and it no longer seemed important whether we would reach our destination before nightfall as I stared, still numbed, from the opposite bank at the treacherous river which had so nearly claimed our lives.

"You have arrived!" said the manager of the sugarcane factory where we were to spend the night. "Many are swept to their death at that river," he went on. He had appeared at the heavily barred gate to let us in, a quietly-spoken impressive man who wasted no words of greeting at the late hour of our arrival. He swiftly handed me over to a servant and invited the Brahman to be his guest.

It was not the season for hauling in the sugarcane and the barn I was taken to was a vast empty space rising twenty feet high to the eaves. A dim light came from a hole under the eaves, a shaft from the starry sky which traced the outline of a narrow bed and a single water tap against the opposite wall. Thankful simply to be alive, I fell into a deep sleep, utterly exhausted from our traumatic experience, to be woken by a fierce dawn piercing the aperture. Shortly after, the same servant reappeared, bringing a cup of tea and a slice of bread on an old brown tray. It had been an eerie resting place, with no toilet facilities but for a mean flow from the tap; and as I looked around the large empty barn, imagined it bustling with activity during the cane crushing season, I thought it had served me well enough as a night stop. But I was desperate to be gone, impatient for the Brahman to finish his full breakfast.

Our aim had been to reach the sacred city of Puri where my revered guide and I were to part company; but we had another night's stop ahead of us. We were now travelling in hostile country, barren lands inhabited by cobras; and I had been left at a rundown inspection bungalow, while the Brahman slept elsewhere. The bungalow was deserted except for a watchman, a withered bent old man who spoke of better days in the service of the British Resident.

All the signs were of decay – the peeling walls, a long-faded portrait of George V and Queen Mary hanging lopsided from a broken hinge. What predatory creatures inhabited these crumbling walls, I wondered fearfully. The watchman covered the table with a cloth of fine Irish linen stained with age and brought a simple meal he had cooked himself.

V. S. Naipaul, who ranks among the world's greatest travel writers, when travelling in India in 1962 had had similar experiences away from the main centres, which he describes as hard. "In some places you spent the night in a room in a railway station," he writes. "In some places, if you could get the official permission that was required, you stayed at a 'dak'(bungalow). It was a lovely name, suggesting old-fashioned travel, and old-fashioned attentions. But when you got to the sunstruck, mildewed, colonial bungalow you had to shout for the watchman; and eventually some barefoot ragged fellow appeared and offered to cook for you in the kitchen of his own quarters the kind of meal he cooked for himself, which, when it came, might smell of woodsmoke or the cowdung cakes over which it had been cooked. In the sparsely furnished bedroom the coarse-napped bedding would smell of the brackish or tainted soapy water in which it had been washed; the floor would feel sandy or gritty underfoot; the mosquito net would have tears and holes; the ventilation gaps at the top of the wall would leave one feeling exposed. The night could feel long."

In 1961 I had listened to the watchman in the bungalow in which I was staying. He had said: "People here are poor and angry. But the British Resident had kept peace with them. He was a strange man, always dressed for dinner. Had the table laid with fine china and glass each evening to entertain distinguished guests. Then sat alone in full evening dress, his decorations upon his chest."

I did not sleep well that night.

Next day we reached the sacred city of Puri where a *Puja* was taking place, a festival of oblations to a deity, flowers, garlands, saffron, dedicated before the holy image. The Brahman had reached his spiritual home. But there was the matter of the Brahman's fee for our journey together.

"My calling is to teach and to teach without payment," he had said with an air of one who despises money; and he pulled from his garment a sheet of paper. "I am in need of these books," he ran his finger down a long list he had penned. "You can purchase them in Puri and leave them at your hotel." And he had joined the crowd of pilgrims. It was the last I saw of my erudite guide. I was quite sorry to see him go. I had come to rely on his pious certainties: "We are expected. We will arrive." And so we did, through high water and low.

Soon I would be continuing with a new guide on a very different journey.

But that night I was to enjoy the sheer luxury of nearby Gopalpur's *Oberoi Palm Beach Hotel* – a blazing icon of global tourism far removed from that other India of destitute families squatting on railway platforms. There was a fresh bite in the air, which dispelled the heat and dust of our travels; and a calm blue sea with silver sands stretching the Bay of Bengal – an untroubled tranquillity at every turn.

Meenakshi, had she been here, would have retreated to the shrines of Puri. Instead, I wallowed shamelessly in a warm bath, dined well and slept in blissful comfort.

Nityanand called next morning, a friendly broad-shouldered man in his mid-thirties. He had been a pupil of the British anthropologist, Fred Bailey, who first lived among the Konds, tribals of the Orissa highlands; and we were to travel together to visit 'Bailey's village'. Nityanand's excitement was electric as he traced from a map the tortuous jungle route.

"But we have a problem," Nityanand had said. "My driver will not go into these tribal areas without a second vehicle in case of a breakdown. He says the wild men up there are dangerous and there are tigers and bears."

With two drivers, two station wagons and six guards, we set off in convoy for Lenkudipara inspection bungalow at the foot of the Kondmals, an extension of the Eastern Ghats some five hundred metres above sea level. This was to be our base but we found the bungalow deserted, the gates securely locked, and lost some time locating the watchman.

We had arranged ourselves in the two-room bungalow and called

North Indian dry land farmer off to the fields.

East Indian women transplanting rice seedlings thrown to them off the cart.

for food: three large pans of steaming gruel flavoured with various spices eventually arrived, each with a long-handled spoon for serving. We gathered round the pans which had been set on a crude wooden table and Nityanand was the first to dip in. I went to follow but was immediately shouted down. "You are forbidden to touch this pot," Nityanand cried, pointing to the one in the middle. "It will be defiled by your hand." The inviolable laws of Hinduism, of clean and unclean, had prevailed.

At dawn, we began the difficult trek into the tribal heartland as the rising sun lifted the shrouding mists off the mountain peaks. Spectacular waterfalls glistened through dense jungle to swell the confluence of the Mahanadi River on its journey to the plains and eventual discharge into the Bay of Bengal. The climb was precipitous, treacherous and slow, when suddenly, in a jungle clearing, 'Bailey's village' confronted us; and we were immediately surrounded by an aggressive crowd. It was Nityanand's hurried greeting that allayed their suspicions: we were not Hindu officials from the plains after all and we all shook hands amid excited chattering.

"Some men are in the jungle axing down trees and burning for planting seeds," Nityanand had interpreted. "They are pointing to spirals of smoke. Some of the women are far in the jungle, too, collecting roots and berries. They say we should come back tomorrow and there will be feasting."

But as we toured the village, presented gifts we had brought with us, I was struck by the different physical features of the villagers from those of the Hindus; and in their dress, their mud huts, their style of living. I felt as though I had 'dropped out of the skies into Africa'; and thought a belief by some pre-history visionaries that migrants from India had populated Africa might have had some truth.

The return journey to our bungalow base took less time than it had to reach the village; and we had not seen a tiger. We were feeling good – till we rounded a bend into the bungalow gates. Strewn over the ground in front of the bungalow was our baggage, some of the contents spilling out. Who had vandalised the place? The door was ajar. Nityanand sprang from our vehicle in a rage and went inside.

Suddenly our second vehicle roared off taking with it the six guards. Nityanand, at the sound, rushed out again, grabbed our driver and took the car keys. "There are twenty military inside," he cried. "Do you want to be shot!" And he turned to me. "They are accusing you of smuggling alcohol."

Suddenly the commanding officer came forward: slowly, he thumbed through my passport, while I inwardly trembled that I might not receive it back. And when at last he handed it back, there was a price to pay. We were told we had entered a prohibitied area. Nityanand interpreted: "There has been trouble with illegal possession of alcohol at the new giant Hindustan Steel Plant at Rourkela north of the state and they searched through our baggage. Now we are being accused of entering a tribal area without a police licence. We have been ordered to leave immediately for the state capital Bhubaneswar." And as we drove away, utterly relieved to be gone, Nityanand went deeper into the conflicting interests of the region. "The Hindus are trying to demolish tribal customs," he said. "They want to integrate 'these backward people', as they call the tribal minorities, into Hindu society. It has become a sensitive political issue."

It was time for Nityanand and I to part company.

We had reached Bhubaneswar without further incident – a fantastic modern city overlooking old Bhubaneswar with its five hundred surviving temples crammed in narrow streets out of the many thousand that date from between the eighth and the thirteenth centuries. We had wandered through the wide clean streets of new Bhubaneswar with its impressive Academy of Science and Technology and the Arts dominating the skyline; and stopped to admire exquisite pastel paintings by a pavement artist of Hindu mythology. There was an exhilarating air of briskness and energy among the city dwellers as we moved toward the railway station.

And I took the super-fast express for Calcutta.

Some seven hours later, the train pulled into Calcutta's Howrah Station to the seething platform multitude of the wretched homeless. Cradle of Mother Teresa's home for the destitute, Calcutta owes its rapid growth from a small village to its choice in 1690 by the East India Company for a warehouse. Historically, however, the city is more usually remembered for the infamous 'black hole massacre' of 1756, when one hundred and thirteen Britons were imprisoned in a single room and died of suffocation; and 'Clive of India's' subsequent defeat of the Nawabs of Bengal and Oudh in 1774, when Calcutta became the capital of British possessions. In 1911, the capital was moved to Delhi.

Calcutta has been called the 'city of dreadful night'; but it should not be missed by any traveller who seeks to find the varied facets of Indian reality.

CHAPTER 11

THE 'HOMECOMING'

The highlight of my India travels had been our surveys in Tamil Nadu of villages first studied in 1916 by Professor Gilbert Slater's Madras University students, again in 1936 by one of those students, and again in 1961 by Meenakshi and me. I had been so inspired by the importance of these surveys that early in 1962, two months after leaving Calcutta, I was back in Jenyr, the Gambia village we had left twelve years earlier; and I had been rejoined by Ebou.

The question which had arisen in my mind was: "What had been happening during those years?" Experience of the Slater surveys had demonstrated that 'village societies' are not static, that the one-off study will soon be relegated to the annals of history.

Today, Britain's African colonies were on the verge of collapsing like a pack of cards. The Gold Coast had already gained independence and had renamed itself Ghana.

It was like a homecoming. This time the flight had taken only two days from London, with a fascinating night stop in the Canary Islands. And Ebou was waiting at Yundum airport, still the same barn-like wooden building and disorganised reception, baggage flung on a bench outside, bursting its sides on impact. And it was off to Bathurst to pick up a truck and begin our slow crawl on rocky outcrops and bush paths up-country for Jenyr.

Imagine our surprise when we finally reached Jenyr. In every village we had passed through we had been hailed by chattering, laughing children running after us, trying to jump on to the vehicle, men and women hurrying to greet us as we passed through, when at last Jenyr village came into view. We felt a sudden emotion in anticipation of a huge welcome.

Nothing moved. The village was silent. Had the villagers fled? Had they been afflicted by some disaster? Ebou went cautiously to the Alkali's

Jenyr women leaving the village to work in the rice swamp.

Bringing in the rice harvest – men head-loading bundles placed along the causeway for transfer to the village store.

Thick mangrove forest lining the Gambia River (salt part of the year), which absorbs salt. The annually-flooded swamp behind the mangrove has been transplanted, with rice yielding a rich harvest to the edge of the mangrove forest (see above). (Today, through mindless slashing for building material of the vital mangrove forest, invading salt pans have rendered the once productive rice swamps infertile with loss of a staple food.)

The total village groundnut harvest (peanuts), piled in the sun to dry, is being put into bags by the growers before being weighed and priced by the representative of the Gambia Marketing Board.

compound and disappeared from sight.

It was uncanny. It was in flabbergasting contrast to the loud welcomes in the villages we had so recently passed through, the dust flying up under the trample of feet as people rushed to greet us. Somewhat relieved, I saw Ebou coming back with the Alkali.

"Everyone is afraid," Ebou said. "You have come to claim your land. You remember you took machines into the forest and cleared away all the trees."

"That was an experiment in land clearing. It does not make it my land."

"In this country," said Ebou, "the first person to clear land from forest is the perpetual owner of that land."

"Tell the Alkali I have not come back to claim my land. The land belongs to the village. I have come on a friendly visit after all these years."

Ebou translated. And the Alkali's face suddenly lighted up like a beacon. He took my hand in both his in a fierce grip, welcomed me back to the village and called his people hiding in their huts, crying out the 'good news'. Instantly, every one was jostling around us shouting praises. And when the Alkali invited us to walk over to Haswell's land, five hundred villagers came crowding along.

All at once there it was, the fifty-acre block we had cleared of forest with the aid of a tractor and blade twelve years earlier; today a stunning sight, young green shoots jostling for space over the entire fifty acres, straining to reach the tropical sun's parcel of energy.

The timing of this second visit to Gambia had been propitious. Momentous things were happening. The colonial administration was about to pack its bags. The battle for an interim self-governing administration was on the boil. Ebou had gone to stay with Jarju, his close friend in Jenyr. I had taken over an unoccupied expatriate mud and thatch house in Massembe village, a mile from Jenyr. It had a history. It had been built, with equipment storage facilities attached, to house an expatriate engineer hired by Bill in that first flush of post-War enthusiasm for replacing the hand-hoe with tractors.

The house, isolated from the rest of the village, had stood empty for the past five years. I had hired a house boy and cook and settled in to witness the most extraordinary events. Could these angry people be the simple tribal folk I had lived among for three years? A band of women were waving a red rag fixed on a long stick and shrieking "Vote for PPP". That same night, two Jenyr compounds were burnt to the ground because they housed visiting campaigners touting for the opposing party, the party of Bathurst, stronghold of western-style descendants of returned slaves from America's Deep South.

Suddenly, from my mosquito-netted window, I saw a white man grab a black boy. Stick in hand he was about to thrash the boy. "Stop!" I ran out calling.

"This black boy has stolen my cigarette."

"Leave the boy alone and go!" I said. And as I watched him slope off I thought how sad the remnant of white people were, mainly post-war contractors with no allegiance to Africa, the Africa of dedicated colonial officers – Oxford and Cambridge men sent to Trinidad to prepare for a career in a tropical country, who had been posted as resident district commissioners living among – and deeply attached to – the local community they served.

Late in the day there had been a rush to develop Gambian infrastructure. A tarred road had replaced the rough Bathurst highway leading out of the capital. And Ebou and I had gained the benefit of it for a third of the way as we travelled up to Jenyr. But the ferry crossing over a tributary of the river still depended on the self-same antiquated creaking structure hand pulled by a steel rope; crocodiles lurking in the water below. Another twenty miles of rocky bush track and suddenly Jenyr came into sight.

We had been surprised at the changed layout of the village. No longer were there a few scattered mud huts. Today, many more were neatly lined along the sandy village path. And causeways had been built across the rice swamps with bundles of recently hand-cut rice lining the banks. It had been a bumper harvest. A donkey cart was plying from the village to the edge of the swamp receiving the bundles as they were head-loaded along the causeways, which saved the head-loaders the extra half-mile walk right into the village. And on the sandy uplands, a bumper harvest of the cash crop groundnuts was waiting to be threshed, grown on land, the Alkali proudly told us, which had been ploughed using donkeys instead of the hand-hoe.

But we were hearing from angry elders how the young men were breaking away from their traditional extended families and building houses of their own. The elders were grumbling at the loss of family labour, the Alkali had said.

It had been an exciting time to return to Jenyr. The village and its environs had markedly gained from the colonial government's latter-day impetus to develop the country's infrastructure and improve its food and livestock. But now the villagers were all fired up in the political wrangle. Jenyr to a man was supporting the Peoples Progressive Party, the party of the rural upcountry. And much blood was being spilt in nightly 'political war-cries' with tribal overtones.

CHAPTER 12

DEMONS IN THE SHADOWS

The administrations of newly-independent countries of Africa and Asia were sending men and women to Oxford on 'how to run a government' courses. Exchanges of ideas rollercoastered between nationals of different cultures and unlikely friendships flourished. Oxford University had opened its doors to the wider world. It was a time of optimism, opportunity and high expectation. While running courses and giving lectures on tropical economics to overseas students, I had been awarded a South East Asia Treaty Organization Fellowship; and, in 1969, I began my travels as a SEATO Fellow, first visiting East Pakistan, renamed Bangladesh at the break between East and West Pakistan.

I had arrived in Dacca, the capital of East Pakistan, a large Deltaic plain in the heart of monsoon Asia, in the season of high rainfall. Lying in the basins of the Ganges, the entire landscape as far as the eye could see was submerged in flood waters. People were struggling to the tops of houses, cattle were drowning, a million tons of rice were being destroyed and there were heavy losses of jute. In the midst of this distressing sight, I left Dacca by light aircraft to a point where I could take a boat across the river to visit the Ganges-Kobadak scheme in Kushtia District, where the control and development of water resources was in early stages of completion. But I had been unprepared for the hostility of other travellers on the boat – a party of overpowering middle-aged Muslims with unnerving stares muttering "infidel". On reaching Kustia, I was already feeling desperate in this strange unwelcome place which would offer me no accommodation when, out of the blue, a young Englishman came to my rescue and told a reluctant hotel proprietor he would be handing his room over to me. With immense relief and unspeakable gratitude, I asked him where he would sleep? He said: "I am going back to England tomorrow. I can kip down anywhere." Next morning, I visited the unfinished Ganges-Kobadak irrigation works; and peasants at its perimeter struggling to survive on tiny plots of land where little rain fell.

Map of East Pakistan
(later renamed Bangladesh at partition from West Pakistan).

Back across the river and waiting, the sole passenger for the return flight to Dacca, I asked the only official at the grassy airstrip what he was doing up a turret: "Shooting the birds as the plane comes in," he had replied. And so he did, with a terrifying happy-go-lucky series of explosions around the cockpit.

On the broad steps of the Bureau of Economics in the University of Dacca where I was to join Dr Farouk the Director, I had been accosted by angry beggars, which had brought sharply home East Pakistan's nightmare exodus from India. At Independence, the new frontier of East Pakistan had been left with the hurried influx of thousands of Muslims – and pressing problems: Calcutta on the Indian side had all the railway workshops; jute mills were all on the Indian side but the jute fields were on East Pakistan's side. Industries, engineering, building and transport were all on the Indian side, and medicine relied on the big Calcutta hospitals for serious cases. All technical education was in India.

I took a flight to West Pakistan where I was to give a talk – a thousand miles from its eastern partner over Indian territory. But East Pakistan's western 'neighbour' lived in terrain where camels were harnessed to carts and the dust blew into one's face. Men were proud and disdainful, and I discovered I had travelled to speak only to their eastern compatriots living among them. It had seemed even at that distance that the two wings of Pakistan, so widely apart in territory, climate and culture, would eventually break away to become two nations: Pakistan and Bangladesh.

My onward journey to Thailand as a SEATO Fellow had been only my first of several visits. I had arrived in Bangkok, captivated by the charm and friendliness of the people in this garish, exuberant, bewitching capital city, the breathtaking temples, the klongs (canals) which drifted amiably along the side of streets.

The writer Graeme Wilson had just expressed his feelings in a tantalising poem. *The road, canal and railway, run north in parallels through floes of water-hyacinth and villages of bells; bells of an aqueous beauty whose tenor tidings flow in smaller spurts to smaller pools the further north you go, until they tinkle in a cess where sun and silence cram into a single knowlessness…* But as I left Bangkok, travelling in a station wagon accompanied by an interpreter, passing through the rich rice-growing central plain of the Chao Phra river and reaching the dry northeast, I was gripped by the memory of a verse written by the

Market day in a Northeast Thailand town .

Packing away the baskets at the end of a good day at the market.

playwright Bertold Brecht, which so aptly described the scene before us. It ran like this: *I keep yelling 'Buy my water.' But no one's buying, athirst and dying. Can't you hear them shrieking: water!* Sure enough, as we climbed on foot the rough road in the northeast village of Roi Et looking for a night's lodging, we were shouted at by an angry young man who had lost a leg: "You'll find nothing here. You got to get out or you die," he had said. And the further we travelled away from the rich rice delta of the Central Plain, the more destitute were the villagers – still, in this age of modern machinery, using primitive wooden ploughs.

We had been surprised by the sudden appearance of four youths as we were struggling with our vehicle on a wind-blown sandy track. They had jumped into the vehicle and robbed us of the last eight bottles of our Fanta orange drink. We followed them to a group huddled in the shade of a mean building and were mortified at what we saw. An aged seer was passing a mug filled with our Fanta orange to rows of children, all kneeling. Each child was being given a sip. It was very moving; but our interpreter had been quick to say that the mug was Chinese and that the seer's blue cotton garment was Chinese. So we left them to it and carried on our way.

External influences were filtering into the country. We had continued northeast to northernmost Nongkai on the mighty Mekong River to torrential downpours of rain. On the opposite bank shone the bright lights of Vientiane. Here, we had bribed our way into the only hostelry, which was heaving with military. The atmosphere was treacherous. Gunshots and sudden screams kept us wakeful through the long night.

We left Nongkai for the American base at Udon, perilously driving through flooded streets, weaving between floating corpses of animals. But we had not gone far when we were flagged down by an armed patrol – a nerve-wracking exchange at the point of a gun. The delay ran us into darkness and on reaching the American base we were dazzled by the bright lights; smart American servicemen were strolling among street vendors, a local girl on each arm. All the amenities at the hotel we had booked into were Western. It was another world, a world which seemed deeply to offend *where sun and silence cram into a single knowlessness*…

I returned to Bangkok for a flight to the Philippines – my final destination as a SEATO Fellow. But there was no direct flight to Manila and I had to change planes in Saigon (renamed Ho Chi Minh City after the Vietnam War).

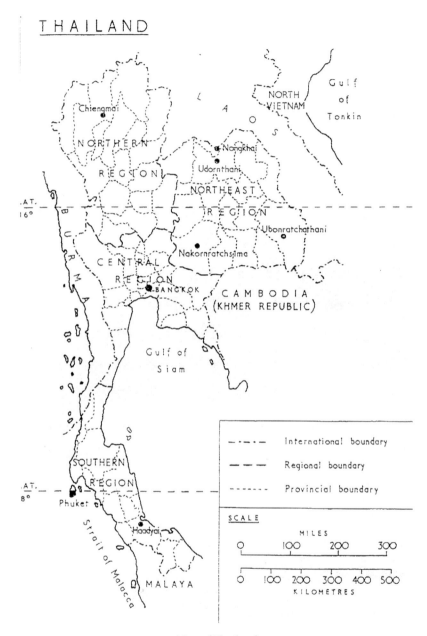

Map of Thailand.

The Air France jet soared relentlessly out of Bangkok into Vietnam carrying GIs we had so recently seen casually sauntering in a secure haven which was *their* America, *their* homeland transported to a parcel of Thai soil. A dreadful gloom had descended upon the GIs. "All these American guys want is to go home," said a Swiss Red Cross worker sitting beside me. "They thought they were fighting communism," she said. "Instead they have become embroiled in a struggle between national enmities. They are dying for nothing."

On our arrival in Saigon we were handed coupons for purchases: Saigon had no currency. The GIs filed into waiting trucks. A Red Cross vehicle had drawn up for the Swiss lady. As we parted, she thrust into my hand a tortoiseshell paper-knife embossed with a gold emblem at its hilt. Pointing to the cryptic emblem she said: "It means peace!" Then she, too, was gone and I was left alone hoping for an aircraft to arrive bound for the Philippines. I had been given vouchers for meals in lieu of currency which was out of circulation with the Vietnam War raging; but there were no eating places. Then, at last, a solitary plane touched down en route to the Philippines; and my anxieties vanished.

"The Philippines are like a sugar cube slowly dissolving on the edge of a saucer of hot coffee," said the pilot lightheartedly as we left Saigon for Manila. "Seven thousand isles scattered like pearls flung by a legendary

POST-GRADUATES AT OXFORD: home from field research in Uganda and Sarawak (author in centre).

goddess into the empty sea," he had said poetically – I his only passenger. "In 1898," he went on, "the Americans conquered the Philippines after three hundred years under Spanish rule, but a promise to grant her independence was dashed by the Japanese invasion of the Philippines in World War II – and in 1945 at the end of the War America abruptly pulled out leaving chaos and confusion." We were about to descend and reluctantly I had to return to my seat. But he had had one last word: "Four centuries of colonial rule and invasions have left the Filipinos spineless." And with his words still ringing in my ears, I arrived at the Mabuhay on Mabini Street in downtown Manila.

It was like a funfair. Milling crowds occupied the street in competition with honking 'jeepneys', their streamers of coloured ribbons whipping the garish painted sides of these once American army jeeps. The carnival atmosphere was breathtaking. I had arranged to meet Teddy and his young wife Felice at the hotel. Teddy had been a student at Oxford and they had burst into the hotel lobby with a thunderous welcome. "We've fixed lunch at the Little Munchen across the street," Teddy said. "Cora, Corazan, Catalina and Oscar are joining us. Quite a reunion," he laughed.

They had all been on courses at Oxford; back home they had lost touch. So the excitement, the chatter, was infectious as they burst into the Munchen. Cora and Corazan were typically Spanish, expansive and jolly who you might expect to fling themselves into the country's spirited *Bayanihan* music and spectacular dance. Catalina was different, the small, neat figure of a Filipino-Chinese. And Teddy was from another ethnic group altogether. He was from the Ifugao, a traditional head-hunting tribe from the remote cold mountains north of Manila.

"You have to see our famous rice terraces at Banaue," Teddy turned to me. "They are said to be the eighth wonder of the world. Cut out of the mountain sides by my Ifugao tribal people three thousand years ago," he puffed out his chest in pride.

"Is it far from Manila?" I asked, wondering how I might make the journey into the mountains.

"None of us have ever been to the famous rice terraces," said one of the girls. "But I'd like to go," Catalina cried excitedly.

"It's a three hundred mile trek to the north from here in Manila," Teddy said as if it were child's play, but added that the climb was hairy. "You'll need to hire a four-wheel-drive vehicle and a driver. But you cannot leave our country without seeing our famous rice terraces," he urged, when Catalina chipped in.

"We could travel together," she said, panting to come along.

And so Catalina and I left Manila for the long haul to the mountain province in the extreme north, aiming for the famous Banaue rice terraces. Andres, the jeep driver, was a little Filipino who had never travelled far from Manila and could only speak Tagalog, the national language; no sooner had we pulled out of Manila than he began to see demons in every passing shadow like an elf.

"I guess he's afraid of the Huks," Catalina said.

"Who are the Huks?" I asked.

"After the War and the invading Japanese had gone, we were left with quantities of discarded army equipment available to any band of guerrillas," Catalina said. "And there was a massive peasant uprising against the landlords right here who had oppressed the peasants for centuries. The landlords own vast *haciendas* which they jealously guard with private armies. See there?" she pointed. "That's Mount Arayat, the most dangerous communist hideout in the country. The communists have exploited the Huks and it has become difficult to distinguish between desperate peasants and ideological communist rebels."

Andres put his foot hard on the accelerator and we raced nervously on till we reached Baguio city – and we were in a world apart, wonderfully cool after the oppressive Manila heat. "We are self-sufficient in almost all our needs," said a friendly passerby. "We trade with the mountain tribes." But for us as we left Baguio city for the treacherous mountain trails, it was a very different matter.

Andres struggled to keep to the winding narrow track, the vehicle's lights picking out towering mountain slopes and deep ravines in the enshrouding blackness when, to our relief, we came upon an old hunting lodge. We were over seven thousand feet into the mountains and it was cold. The proprietor was the sole occupant. The rooms were rambling, with old-fashioned furnishings and no heating. But in a barn-like room below a welcome log fire burned and we were entertained, with draughts of *basi,* the local beer, to an evening of tribal music the proprietor played on his bamboo blowpipe. As we set off again next morning, he warned us of the hazardous track ahead with the cheerless news that only the previous week two Americans had met their deaths falling into a ravine.

We had just rounded a hairpin bend when a massive fall of rock thundered down in front of us. "My God!" Catalina cried. To our right we stared into a deep bottomless ravine. To our left mountains reared perpendicular. Andres began hurling rocks into the ravine like a madman. We were alone. No 'mobiles' in those days. Nothing for it but to abandon the vehicle and crawl back along the dangerous mountain track. But Andres, with superhuman strength, had finally cleared a space and began to edge his vehicle through as we watched, holding our breath. Utterly relieved, on we scarily crawled round ever more hairpin bends, when suddenly an unimaginable panoramic view sent us reeling. Before our eyes spread the world famous Banaue rice terraces, giant steps cut into the mountains circling to the horizon, pools of water gleaming in the treads where rice had grown for many centuries, the hidden wonder of an ancient and proud mountain people, the Ifugao miracle.

To celebrate our safe return from the Banaue rice terraces, we joined Teddy and friends for dinner at Manila's Intramuros, arena of the city's ancient walled fortress built by the Spaniards in the sixteenth century on the site of a village settlement – today, a haunt of the rich and famous. Hugging the walls in the stifling heat, we watched an open-air theatre show, while easy-going fun-loving Manilans made hospitable overtures. It was Sunday and the mood was festive, romantic, carefree, aimless – "a kind of betrayal," Teddy had said. "We ignore the Tondo slums outside our wealthy city piled high with garbage, where a million poor live in cardboard shanties," he had said as we wandered through Rizal Park close by Intramuros.

Images of a city in turmoil sat uneasily as I left Manila for Cebu, the city Manilans called 'Queen of the South'. Arriving in Cebu city, hub of the Visayan Islands, no more than an hour's flight from Manila, was to take a step back in time. Here it was that Ferdinand Magellan, the Portuguese adventurer who ignobly served his country's arch rival Spain, landed in 1521 while sailing the seas for the rich trade in spices; and decided to settle and convert to Christianity the heathen tribes he found living on the island. A year later, in a display of Spanish military might, he became embattled with a wild tribe living on nearby Mactan Island and was killed by its chief, Lapu-Lapu, with all but one of his ships scuttled. For almost fifty years after this affray, little interest was shown in the Philippines. It was left to the sagacious Miguel Lopez de Legaspi to bring permanent Spanish settlement when he stormed Cebu Island in 1565. On old Colon Street, where Magellan had first stepped foot, the

Magellan shrine said to contain fragments of the cross he had used in his conversions to Christianity buzzed with tourists. Proudly, a guide was pointing to an image of Jesus as a child, given, he told admiring visitors, in 1521 by Magellan to Queen Juana of Cebu on her baptism. Today, a sense of Philippine history pervades the city, the anachronism of this fiercely Catholic country incongruously amidst the ancient religious cultures of Southeast Asia.

A short hop and I had flown from rich historic Cebu Island into Bacolod on Negros Island for a visit to Victorias Milling Company, one of the world's largest sugar refineries, to be shocked to find a 'hidden feudalism' extant. I had been taken to visit one of the wealthiest sugar barons on the island, a man in his prime, of immense girth and height, his bearded face disguising the thin line of his mouth, his eyes cold and calculating. Around his waist he wore a broad leather belt, on each side of which a pistol jutted from a holster. He and I left his luxury residence in an armour-plated, four-wheel-drive vehicle. Fifteen minutes later we pulled into a vast field of sugarcane that stood ten feet high. We stepped out and began to walk toward the cane cutters, cane falling like giant broken reeds at their feet as they ferociously slashed, when suddenly one of the cutters turned at our approach and raised his cutting arm poised to strike. In a flash the sugar baron had both pistols aimed. Still the cane cutter pinned us with eyes full of hate; and I had turned and walked slowly back to the vehicle, praying that the sugar baron would not fire his pistols.

Later, at tea as a guest of Victorias Milling, a waiter said: "You take sugar Ma'am?" and handed white sugar lumps in a bowl of fine China. And I thought how far those icy glistening sugar lumps have travelled from the hell of the cane cutters' task – so many people across oceans ignorant of the pain of it, the sugar barons' harvest.

And so, with mixed feelings, I left the Visayan Islands for Cagayan de Oro on Mindanao, the remote southern and second largest island of the Philippine archipelago. Locally named 'city of gold' for its thriving pineapple estates, this prosperous university town gave no hint of the island's troubled civil war. I had been joined on the flight by Prissy Lapuz, a native of Mindanao, brown-skinned, beak-nosed, eagle-eyed, who might in earlier times have worn a chieftain's headdress and drawn a bow. We had been shocked to hear that the plane due to land after ours had been blown up with no survivors; thirty innocent passengers had died for the assassins to get at one man. It was a sobering thought – but for the grace of God…

We had set off for Wao, a 200 km gruelling journey where no roads existed but waterlogged forest tracks, in a four-wheel-drive vehicle, to meet Christian migrants from the Visayas who had settled on land which Muslim Moro tribesmen were claiming as rightfully theirs; and we were entering troubled territory off-limits to tourists. While typhoons devastate the northern islands with unpredictable ferocity and little warning, Mindanao Island escapes this wrath of the elements. But for all the superior forces of the Spanish in every century of their presence, this bastion of Islam could not be subdued; and later when American generals tried to implant their flag, Moro tribes angrily tore it from the soil, crying: "This land is ours, always has been, always will be."

In the wake of a particularly ferocious attack by Moro tribesmen, land reform officers settling Christian migrants in Wao had taken cover in a large wooden barn. Forewarned by 'bush telegraph' that we were about to descend upon them, they had prepared a feast of wild game. Welcomed by the mayor, we took our seats at a trestle table along with seventeen local workers, each of whom had placed their gun beside their plate, to be told that Lapuz and I were to travel a further twenty miles to Banisilan as soon as the meal was over, where we would be staying.

A rusty jeep left over from World War II drew up and Lapuz chained me into the passenger seat. "We are expecting an ambush," he said, and crouched on the running-board beneath me, pointing his gun at the rolling terrain.

"The Christians are getting out because of tribal conflict," said the driver. "Lots of these government-sponsored settlers are city guys from Manila and they are fleeing. Out of the first hundred families settled in Banisilan, only three are left."

"There's a new wave of settlers coming from nearby islands," shouted Lapuz from his crouched position. "Peons escaping from the sugar barons."

And all the while we kept on the alert for raiding tribesmen. But there was nothing. The shock came as we approached Banisilan. Encamped five hundred yards apart, two great crowds had gathered – Muslim tribes from the mountains and forests to our left; to our right, Christian immigrants. Standing alone between these two electrifying gatherings, the Banisilan Land Authority officer was waiting.

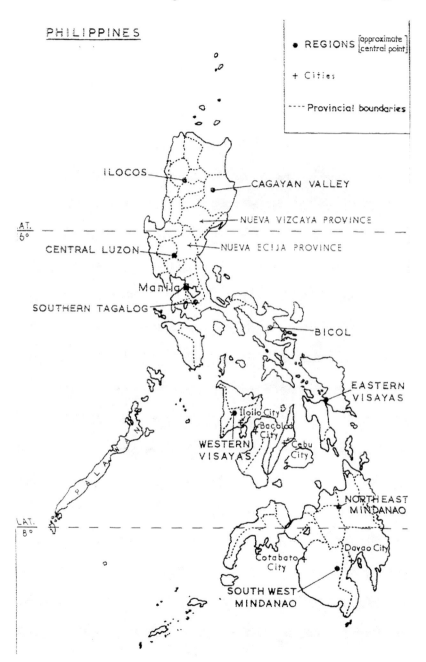

Map of The Philippines.

"Francisco they call me," he said and held out his hand. "As you can see, news of your visit has travelled far. No one ever comes this way." He shaded his eyes under his sombrero, looked toward the Muslim encampment, and said: "Nine datus with several hundred of their Moro tribesmen poured into Banisilan this morning – and not a shot was fired!"

We could feel the tension. "The settlers were dead scared," Francisco had said. "I immediately confronted the chief of the Moro tribes who assured me his followers only wished to pay homage to the foreign visitor. It has been agreed tonight the Moro tribes will provide entertainment. Tomorrow will be the turn of the Christians." He wiped the sweat from his brow with a large handkerchief. "A peaceful presence of Muslims in Banisilan? Pray God there'll be no bloodshed!" he had said as he showed me to a barn he had had turned into a bedroom for my use.

The first evening was a fantastic display. An area had been cordoned off and we had watched a spectacular performance. The Muslim tribes had staged a mock battle, spurring their horses in a javelin game. Young girls in exquisite costume had paraded in front of us, paying homage to their revered chief, when suddenly he rose up and requested photographs of his dancers, of his horsemen, and of himself and myself together – a courtesy which, in the event, had unimaginable consequences, involving a death threat. Further, on retiring to the barn after the performance, I found the walls had been decorated with swords, knives, jewelled emblems of conquests, and laid on the floor a thick carpet of fabulous colours. Sitting upon the carpet were three beautiful young women exquisitely dressed; nearby a bowl of fruit had been placed. I tried in vain to communicate with them and wondered how long they would stay.

Next morning, the barn was stripped of all vestiges of Muslim artefacts and the large party of tribes had stolen away under cover of the night. They had had no intention of staying for the Christian settlers' evening which, by contrast, had had a marked simplicity, a few dances and song performed by disparate people yet to find a common identity – so many escaping peonage on the haciendas of the sugar islands only to find it hard to build a homestead with their bare hands.

With much on our minds, Lapuz and I left Banisilan for Wao. There we parted and I began a 216 km jeep journey with a new driver along terrible, deep rutted, disused logging trails. Late in the day, we arrived back at Cagayan de Oro to take up an invitation to visit the Del Monte pineapple plantation. Then, the long flight back to Manila and I had the important film taken in off-limits Banisilan put into the diplomatic bag for safe-keeping to London via Bangkok. It never arrived. It had been stolen from the diplomatic bag!

"From which country's diplomatic bag I wonder it was stolen?" said a friend in the Diplomatic Corps.

A year on and I decided to pay another visit to that troubled southern island of the Philippines. I had been in Mexico, like the Philippines a Catholic country, and been lucky in Mexico City to stay with American friends who introduced me to Mexico's amazing pre-history. But I had been struck by the city's parallel with Manila in the Philippines – widespread urban squatters rummaging through mountains of refuse to scratch a living. I had joined a Mexican to meet some of the corn farming peasants whom we saw riding bareback on horses as we drove past. We had been invited to a fantastic meal in a large barn filled with jocular men in cowboy hats and each with a gun. On our way back to Mexico City we ran over and killed a dog. I said we should stop and find the owner. He put his foot on the accelerator: "If we stop they will kill us!" he said.

I left Mexico travelling to Los Angeles on my way to Hawaii, where I was to give a lecture at East-West Center in Honolulu. It was a hugely enjoyable experience, the more so as I was staying with one of the professors – high above the coastline with magnificent views. Except that the day I was to leave for my onward flight to Manila, we forgot about the date-line. I missed the flight. But where could there have been a more wonderful venue to have had to stay for another day? Hardly had I stepped off the plane in Manila and checked into my downtown hotel than I was telephoned by an anonymous caller with a death threat if I did not leave the country within twenty-four hours. It was a grim reminder of the sinister undercurrent of menace that seemed never far from the surface in metropolitan Manila behind the veneer of carefree Filipinos. I had the chilling thought that someone was out there waiting, watching.

Was the caller in the hotel? Had it been he who had stolen my film which contained pictures of Muslim tribes at war with settlers in troubled Mindanao? I spent a sleepless night and then – the room telephone rang again. I picked up the receiver waiting for that voice I dreaded to hear.

"Hello! Your old friend Orosa here. Welcome back."

"Hello!" I said with a relief he could not possibly have known.

"I'll send a car from the President's office to fetch you over for coffee and a chat. You are welcome to keep the car and the driver as long as you are in Manila."

It had been a Godsend. The whole day long I felt relatively safe. I had had a meeting planned with Land Reform officers at their Manila headquarters; and they had been surprised and hugely impressed when I turned up in a limousine like a high-ranking foreign visitor; they simply fell over themselves, recalling my earlier visit a year back. But time was running out. I had been in Manila for nearly twenty-four hours and had to make a dash to the airport. Only when I let the car go and waited for my flight did I scarily look over my shoulder at every passer-by. Was someone out there still shadowing me?

At last I boarded my plane. But I had not taken an international flight out of the country. Instead, I had boarded an internal flight back to troubled Mindanao. I had hoodwinked my assailants!

And there was Lapuz, hand-shaking, hugging and laughing. Together, we revisited tribes still at war against Christian settlers from other islands. And when it was time for me to leave Mindanao Island, instead of returning to Manila, almost a thousand miles from their largest and most southern Isle, I had slipped out of the Philippines on a flight to Sarawak in eastern Malaysia. Here I joined a district officer on a journey into the jungle where Indonesian rebels just over the border sprayed us with gunfire as we travelled. We had been alone on the trail and had decided to continue to meet engaging 'head-hunters'; and participate in the 'rights' of a longhouse feast of snake and other tropical delicacies.

From Sarawak, I travelled on to Sri Lanka (formerly Ceylon) where I had one of my Oxford graduate students doing field work for his thesis – and here again was a country engaged in a long civil war. 'Tamil Tigers', descendants of indentured labour on Ceylon's tea estates brought way back from South India during British rule, were today waging war with the Singhalese for the right to own land.

From Sri Lanka I returned, in thought-provoking mood, to Oxford. So much of Asia I had found facing upheaval and engaging in local wars, in a rapidly changing world.

PART THREE

CHAPTER 13

ROOT OF EVIL UNEARTHED

There had been a subtle change in overseas students coming up to Oxford thirty years on from the end of the Second World War. The day of the colonial overlords was over. A new generation had grown which questioned the 'old guard' who had been servants of the British and were now rulers of their countries. Young men and women, born in a free society, were struggling for an identity. They had seized the torch of a new dawn from the hands of their elders. They were all fired up and ready to make their mark.

And there had been a change in my overseas travel with the upsurge of calls for consultants to cooperate with the new governments of Asia and Africa. I had recently been to Uganda for *Freedom from Hunger* to locate sites for farm schools; and had chanced to be in Kampala on the night a daring Jewish plane touched down at the airport under cover of darkness, rescued fugitive compatriots waiting in the shadows, and took off again before the Ugandans had fully grasped what was happening and begun to shoot. To the regret of the audacious pilots, one Jewish lady had to be left behind as she was in hospital. Two days later, she was reported dead in a revenge killing and became an early victim of Amin's notorious cruel presidency.

It was curious that back in Oxford giving the Michaelmas Term lectures, I should have fallen upon a document bearing upon a cruelty much closer to home. I had visited an aunt, the last of my mother's siblings, and she had asked me to fetch a shawl for her. Hidden in a corner of her drawer I found a faded Will of my great-great-great grandfather. Carefully, I unfolded its fragile pages and began to read the chilling discovery that he had been a rich landowner in America's South Carolina and that he had gained his wealth from rice grown on extensive swamps, gained it with the sweat and toil of black slave labour out of Africa.

Gambia, renamed The Gambia, had had ten years under the presidency of Dawda Jawara, democratically elected at Independence with a comfortable majority by the Peoples Progressive Party (PPP), the party of the rural hinterland; and Ebou and I had decided to pay another visit to Jenyr.

I had been reflecting upon the day I first arrived in Jenyr in 1947, reminded of another of my mother's sisters, who had said "whatever does she want to go to Africa for?". I had not appreciated that there had been a 'conspiracy of silence' – until today. Britain's corporate guilt in the ultimate evil of all time, the transport of thousands of Africans across the Atlantic into slavery, had faded into the annals of history. Suddenly it was immediate, direct and personal, and it seemed to me that it had been no coincidence that I should have had in the last quarter-century an inexplicable rapport with Ebou and with Jenyr villagers.

Ebou and I had arrived in Jenyr to a thunderous welcome. Our journey from Banjul (formerly Bathurst) had been surprisingly pleasant on the new bitumen road which had now reached Jenyr; no potholes, no blinding dust churned up by lorries on rocky, sandy tracks, and how well the village looked – a neat row of mud huts, many with tin roofs replacing traditional thatch. The Alkali, the village head man, had greeted us back enthusiastically, running around gathering everybody together, his distinctive blue robe catching the bright sunlight. Mudbank causeways had been built across the swamp to the mangrove trees at the edge of the river and now the women could reach fertile, higher-yielding, soils to transplant their rice seedlings.

But, on looking deeper, it was clear to us that all was not as glowing as our Jenyr friends would have us believe. The river is tidal and salty during the long dry season, and the women could only grow rice during the short rainy season when the water from the river is fresh and the lush mangrove lining the river bank had absorbed the salt; but the mangrove trees were also providing a favourable environment for mosquitoes biting man; and the forces of malnutrition and parasitic infestation were placing Jenyr villagers at risk. "Our health is poor," said the Alkali gravely. "We are suffering from malaria and other sicknesses."

We had discovered that the more numerous dwelling huts in the village were not all housing immigrants from other parts of the country, as we had thought, but were mainly breakaways from their traditional extensive family households. Some young men, together with their first wives in this polygamous society, were now living in their own place and, as the Alkali had told us, it only needed the man in these small family units to fall sick and be unable to farm for the family to go hungry. Further, many Jenyr mothers were experiencing extremely high death rates in their under-five-year-old children, which was disturbing.

However, Jenyr villagers had gained from adopting the 'new technology' which had arrived earlier in Gambia, ox ploughing. We found there were twenty-four working oxen in the village, owned and rented to others by prominent families, with which they had ploughed favourable upland soils and planted groundnuts – and as far as the eye could see, a thick carpet of fresh green leaf glistened breathtakingly under the hot sun after we had experienced a sharp downpour of tropical rain. An agent from the marketing board in Banjul would come, they said, when the peanuts had been lifted at the end of the rains and heaped to dry. He would price the nuts and arrange for them to be shipped to Europe.

Gone were the days of the 'closed economy' of our first stay in Jenyr in the nineteen-forties when the village was isolated in a canopy of forest from markets and was self-sufficient. What we had seen on this visit was the beginnings of a social breakdown. The new bitumen road had opened the way to the 'bright lights of the city'.

Ebou and I had been staying in the village as guests like distant relations visiting, he with his friend Jarju and I in the household of the district chief. It had been unwise. I had not escaped a sickness which was afflicting Jenyr families – liver damage, a symptom of which is extreme lethargy. Ebou, Jarju and I had been walking across the rice swamp when my legs began to buckle and I lagged behind. I knew at once I had become a victim of Jenyr sickness and that I had to get out of the country quickly or I would be joining the burial site of Jenyr's families under the Baobab tree. I immediately got our truck driver to rush me to Banjul where, on our arrival, I heard to my horror that two visitors, a French diplomat and a Belgian, had been in hospital with this viral hepatitis and that they had just died. A plane was leaving for London that evening and I dashed to the airport – only to find in dismay that the plane was full. Rapidly turning yellow, helpless in the crowded airport among passengers waiting to board, I was suddenly approached by a quietly-spoken Englishman. "You can have my seat," he said. "I'll take the next plane." His gesture had been a priceless gift from a 'Good Samaritan' passing by.

Back in England, I was faced with a long and exhausting illness. A forthcoming visit to the Caribbean en route to participate in an international conference in Brazil had had to be cancelled.

Ebou and I had found Jenyr infested with rats, sanitation that was still primitive, and that water drawn from wells was polluted and unsafe.

Chapter 14

Barbados-over-the-Sea

It was not uncommon to hear an overseas worker remark "the West African is lazy". I had another answer. I had been left so lethargic, so unwilling to raise a hand, that I had been reduced to dictating the manuscript for a book in its entirety over the telephone to my secretary. The endemic sickness on that awful coast, where nature's hordes of 'killer flies' bear relentlessly on the human population, was draining the life-blood of hapless West Africans, of our Jenyr friends, of myself. To give a lecture to Oxford University students for one hour exhausted me for a whole week.

Towards the end of the long year it took for me to be fully recovered, I had accepted an invitation from Sir Arthur Lewis to give a course of lectures in the spring semester at Princeton University. It was a riveting experience, to arrive on the campus of a university with so magical a history – one of the three earliest American universities to be inaugurated before the American War of Independence in 1776, when thirteen states of America's eastern seaboard were colonized by England. Perhaps the greatest joy of living on the campus was the access I had to Princeton's world-famous library, where I could research and read on any or every night up to midnight. For my sojourn at Princeton was double-edged. At the Easter break I took a flight to South Carolina's capital city and drove a hired car to a small town called Georgetown – once the hub of the rice growing industry – and I went in search of my roots, the dynastic plantation family of a fabulously wealthy South Carolina rice planter. I knew I had to return another day, to find out more and to lay a ghost.

In the early hours of a balmy spring morning I said goodbye to friends in Princeton and waited for the limousine which was to take me to New York for the short flight to Barbados-over-the-Sea. It did not turn up and in a frenzy of activity another car hire service was located. The driver was black; and as we travelled we kept up a light-hearted conversation, when suddenly he turned off the highway into a small side street and disappeared. I abandoned any hope of catching my flight.

Like a sitting duck, I recalled that other time on a lonely stretch in an African jungle when suddenly my African driver had stopped, removed the keys and dived into the undergrowth. The noises of the jungle were petrifying and time stood still. When finally he reappeared he was carrying a mattress on his head.

When my American driver reappeared he carried nothing. And without comment we pressed on to the airport, taking in the scenery, overawed by the great Hudson River. With no sense of urgency any longer, I walked into the airport, suddenly to be hustled by officials through the empty departure lounge to the waiting aircraft. Princeton University had telephoned.

It had come as a shock on reaching Bridgetown, capital of Barbados, to find the skyline dominated by a statue of Lord Nelson. But then, this easternmost Caribbean island of the Lesser Antilles jutting out from the Atlantic was historically the first outpost for ships coming from Europe and was heavily defended by the English navy during the colonial wars of the 17th and 18th centuries. To quote Lord Nelson as the Napoleonic Wars of the early 19th century raged, "Neither in the field nor senate shall our West Indian possessions and rights be infringed while I have an arm to fight in their defence or a tongue to launch my voice against the damnable doctrine of Wilberforce…"

At the time of my travels, although Barbados had become a member of the Commonwealth, the majority of her people descendants of African slaves, she had yet to abolish the Monarchy and the Union Jack flying over Bridgetown seemed an anachronism.

Is sugar still king, I had wondered?

I left Bridgetown to find out.

I was met at the Mount Gay Rum Distillery by a charming black gentleman who epitomised the relaxed atmosphere of the country's mainly black society – until we got talking about the history of Barbadian sugar.

He was a fine looking man in his early forties whose benign expression had belied a tense undercurrent of racial awareness. "Unlike our island neighbours who were fought over by Dutch and Portuguese, we had an English heritage from the start," he opened up. "And we had close links with Carolina in North America. The eastern seaboard of America, as you will know, was colonised by the English at about the same time."

"Trafficking in African slaves?" I suggested.

"Rightly so," he said, "and the main supply of African slaves to Carolina was shipped from our island. But I am a fifth generation away from my enslaved ancestors." He paused reflectively. "What grieves us, torments us, is that we are today Barbadians without a name, our identity stripped from us long ago by the white captors of our forefathers. Our genes," he mused, "are the melting pot of West Africa. And we fret and fight over which fragment of that vast space we try to call our own."

I could find no words. The timeless evil he was describing was a curse upon our English heritage, when English gentle folk had acquired a taste for sugar in their tea, blind to the pain and death which had brought it to them.

And it was he who broke the silence. "I am sure you would like to see our cane fields," he said. "Sugar is still king."

We had passed through the sugar cane heartland and reached Jamestown – Holetown on the west coast.

"This is where the earliest English settlers landed," said my companion. "The town was heavily fortified in the Napoleonic Wars."

"Lord Nelson and the English Navy?"

"Quite so. But my African slave forebears had heard of Wilberforce's abolition law in the English Parliament and thought it included freedom for them. In 1816 they rebelled when they found it was not true and set fire to the cane fields. The Easter Rebellion, which the military quickly quashed, leaving several hundred dead and hanging the leaders."

"The Wilberforce Bill of 1807 abolished the traffic in slaves. It took another two generations before Lincoln in America abolished slavery on the plantations in the south," I commented.

"Just across the water and they drew their supplies from here," my companion added.

We had walked a rugged path to Speighstown, south of Holetown, passing decaying Georgian plantation houses, the homes of once prosperous white planters; and the very air seemed loaded with the town's ugly history as a trading port – Little Bristol as it was infamously called.

I had read Barbadian writer Lamming's novel *The Castle of my*

Skin and, as we rested in the shadow of a crumbling Georgian edifice, I was thinking that it will be he and other Barbadian writers, poets and artists who will inspire their fellow black Barbados nationals proudly to take their place in a rapidly changing world – a heritage born in sorrow, filtered, through the passage of time, with threads of gold.

I had travelled to the Caribbean under the umbrella of the ACP countries of the European Community; and I had come upon a note written by Kevin Garrett to his American friends, which read: "There is a strong culinary connection between Barbados and South Carolina, so if you are familiar with Low Country cooking, you will have a good handle on the native cuisine of Barbados – rice and peas and spicy stews."

In 1625, Barbados had been one of the earliest of the Caribbean Islands to be colonized by the English; and it had been the chance appointment in 1671 of Sir John Yeamans, a prosperous Barbados sugar planter, as the first Governor of South Carolina, that had cemented the historical link between Barbados and South Carolina in America. To the hot, humid, malarial, swamps along the banks of the Ashley River and Georgetown in South Carolina, which I had so recently visited during the Easter break while at Princeton, Yeamans had brought African slaves three hundred years earlier from his Barbados estate to clear massive vegetation for a rice plantation.

With much to reflect upon, I left Barbados for the short flight to St Lucia.

CHAPTER 15

THE SPIRIT SOARS

Many years ago, an eminent professor in the University of Oxford invited a distinguished economist from London University to address a group of senior members and students. The visitor's name was Arthur Lewis; nothing out of the ordinary. But when he arrived, to the complete astonishment of the Oxford professor and the attending audience, the visiting professor was black. This was at a time shortly after the Second World War when academic institutions were only just beginning to resurface and exchanges with scholars from other parts of the world were still a rare occurrence. But I had the good fortune to have been one of those students.

Sir Arthur Lewis was born in this Caribbean Island of St Lucia on 23 January (the same day as another eminent St Lucian, the poet and playwright Sir Derek Walcott, both to become recipients of the Nobel Prize). Almost thirty years had passed since Arthur Lewis's address in Oxford; and I had arrived in St Lucia from Barbados following a semester as a visiting lecturer at Princeton University under the aegis of Sir Arthur. My having so recently lectured in the department of one of their country's most brilliant sons was a fabulous passport to entry as an official guest.

That first magical night at my hotel in Castries, the capital, within sight of a towering mountain dropping sheer into the deep water natural harbour, I dined with the Deputy Premier.

"We are still recovering from our last hurricane" he said. "They are quite frequent in our island. They sweep through the banana plantations like a whirlwind, destroying everything in their wake. But it's the little people who suffer."

"Yet St Lucia has stirred the imagination of great writers," I remarked.

"And musicians," he said. "You should be here on St Cecilia's Day.

Sugar-cane grower driving his cart alongside a tall field of sugar-cane.

A happy crowd showing off a remarkable bridge.

It used to be called Discovery Day because we believed our island was discovered by Christopher Columbus. But no one could prove it. So now we call it St Lucy, the patron saint of light – our National Day on 13 December. And we still believe it was the Spanish who first claimed our island."

But who were these little people growing bananas in the valleys of the interior? I joined a local forester and in a four-wheel drive vehicle we left behind the English-speaking coastal region for the French-speaking interior to seek them out. We immediately faced steep mountain tracks out of Castries with scary hairpin bends; when suddenly there they were in a valley below us, crawling up steep slopes to the track, weighty stems of small bananas in bunches of seven apiece on their backs.

They were tough, short, muscular, and they stared up at us with deeply resentful looks. 'Photograph us at your peril' their waving gestures at my camera seemed to be the words they were breathlessly mouthing.

"They speak a French patois," my companion said. "The King of France claimed our island around 1640, ignoring that we were already peopled by Caribs who made repeated attempts to push them out and actually murdered several of their governors. But the English had their eye on the sugar plantations and began a long and bloody fight with the French. Fourteen times our island changed hands in the space of two hundred years before we became a British Crown Colony by the Treaty of Paris."

We had moved on. I had commented that those small banana growers were very likely descendants of Africans from Dahomey, once colonized by the French. I had personal experience of Dahomey way down the West African coast, of the country's dark-skinned, robust, defiantly independent people who produce amazing art work. I had visited their museums in Dahomey (Benin), seen their ancient blood-curdling wall paintings, decapitated heads thrown into cauldrons; had bought an exquisite brass carving of a bent old man. "It is not surprising," I said, "that here in St Lucia, great painters, musicians, writers, Nobel prize winners, flourish where you have so fascinating and diverse a culture."

"And out of the valleys high up the mountains their spirits soar," my companion said.

CHAPTER 16

SURGING VIOLENCE

My stay in St Lucia had been all too short when I left for Georgetown in Guyana for a meeting at the Caribbean Common Market headquarters. After a flight back to Barbados, I joined an international flight with a stopover in Trinidad. Being ignorant of Guyana's chequered history, I had been surprised when all the passengers on the flight disembarked at Port of Spain in Trinidad – all but two men sitting stiffly several rows behind me. Suddenly the air seemed filled with menace.

The landing in Guyana was uneventful but the airport was eerily deserted. The baggage labels belonging to the two men indicated they were UN officials as they hurried through the arrivals lounge. I raced after them and jumped into their taxi. They said nothing.

But hardly had we left the airport when the cab driver pulled up, took the ignition key and disappeared. Still no comment from the two men. I called to mind the words of the passenger seated next to me as he left the plane in Trinidad: "It's scary where you are going," he had said. We waited and we waited, silent and motionless, and when the driver reappeared he just took the wheel and we were on the move again. Arriving at a hotel in the centre of Georgetown, the two men got out. To reach my hotel, the driver said, was a further twenty minutes. Suddenly alarmed at going off on my own, I followed the men into their hotel. It was already dark.

"We have no vacancies," said the porter as the two men booked in to their rooms.

"Then I will stay here in reception," I said. The porter was unhappy but I would not move. And then he relented. He took me to a small windowless room. The bed had not been made up, the bedcovers were dirty, and there was little light. I felt safe for a few hours.

Next morning there was a buzz as people picked up the daily paper. I glanced over someone's shoulder. "Airline pilot shot dead crossing the hotel courtyard to his car…" I read. It was the hotel which had my booking. I took a cab to the British Embassy needing some assurance. But the doors were locked. I pressed hard on several bells, rattled locks, when at last a voice came over the intercom.

"The Caribbean office is ten minutes' walk across the city. The streets are dangerous. They rip everything off you, rings, necklaces. We cannot let you in. We are closed."

I pocketed my watch and walked the 'dangerous mile', all the while dreading the sound of footsteps behind me.

It was odd to discover that Georgetown on the Atlantic was renowned as 'the garden city of the Caribbean'. Even more surprising that the city housed the headquarters of the Caribbean Common Market. "Why not Barbados?" I asked as my friend welcomed my arrival with the open-handed warmth of his native Trinidad.

He swung round in his director general's plush swivel chair. "It's the old story of power struggles between your English forebears and their European rivals," he said. "Clashes in the mid-seventeenth century between Dutch and English adventurers."

He had a beautiful lilting voice and quixotic dancing eyes as he spoke.

"The English finally settled in 1663," he said. "But not for long. By 1667 the Dutch were back. And here is the interesting part. The Dutch ceded New Amsterdam in exchange for this country. Who got the better deal? The English renamed New Amsterdam New York," he laughed. "A century later the British fleet were on the prowl again. They ousted the Dutch who took six years to regain the territory, only to lose it to Britain the next year. By 1814 Britain had colonised the territory and named it British Guyana."

"Was there an indigenous population all the while the English and Dutch were scrapping for possession?" I asked.

"Native Amerindian tribes. The Dutch and English set up trading posts with them in the hills. But the English laid out plantations and shipped African slaves to work them. The soil was poor and very soon the English took their slaves to the coast, carved out new plantations, grew coffee, cotton, and expanded into Demerara sugar. But slavery was abolished in 1834 and the English lost their African slaves who settled on smallholdings. So the English planters brought indentured labour from

India to work on their plantations."

Someone came in with cold drinks. He moved from his desk to an armchair and we chatted about nothing in particular. Suddenly he said: "When the Indians had finished their indentured service they did not go home. They stayed on and today the country is in rebellion. Hindus and blacks confront one another."

"Third and fourth generations from shipment of people across oceans, their roots firmly in the country of their birth," I remarked.

"And a phenomenal growth of the Indian population," said my host. "Since independence in 1966, the country has been in revolt. Indo-Guyanese and Afro-Guyanese in a power struggle. The blacks, headed by Forbes Burnham, have been favoured by the old colonial power. But Cheddi Jagan for the Indians is hotly contesting the blacks. The country is rich in resources but all this political strife is frightening off foreign investors. Poverty, street fighting and crime have taken over."

Again we were interrupted, this time to clear away the empty glasses. My host started for the door. "You'll stay with us," he turned. "I've cancelled your hotel booking." He settled back in his chair.

"What you are describing reminds me of what I had been hearing in a recent visit to Sri Lanka," I said. "Tamil Tiger rebels are fighting the Singhalese for the right to own land – third generation descendants of indentured labour transported from South India in the last century by colonial Britain to work on Ceylon's tea estates. Today, the South Indian descendants in Sri Lanka are producing rich harvests of chillies in Sri Lanka's northern territory."

"I guess there are parallels," he said. "Here in Guyana, descendants of indentured Indian labour have deep roots. Burning cauldrons are exploding in racial disharmony."

I had left Guyana for Port of Spain, this time to disembark and discover the very different carefree life of the people of Trinidad. The streets of the capital thronged with students at the University of the West Indies, sauntering by, drinking coconut milk through a straw straight from the hairy brown nut.

CHAPTER 17

SOMEONE ELSE'S WAR

I had flown back from Trinidad to Brussels to the ACP wing of the European Community, where I discussed my visit to the Caribbean with their Trinidad Representative. He was a large jovial man with a great sense of humour. His residence was spacious and beautifully furnished. We lounged in comfortable chairs and talked at length about the aspirations of his people. As a parting gift, he gave me a fine bottle of Trinidad rum.

It was the heyday for European consultants engaging with African, Caribbean and Pacific policy-makers. But who were they? Many were now wearing a different hat. They had been colonial administrators, district commissioners and the like; now they were advising their one-time employees, who had replaced them at independence.

But these European consultants were more than mere advisers. They collaborated with their former colonial public servants in a range of development programmes.

My Caribbean venture completed, I was about to journey on a new and exciting venture to the Solomon Islands. I would be joining three other consultants – an American, an Australian and a New Zealander, all of us recruited by the Asian Development Bank in Manila. I was now increasingly involved with the upsurge of teams of consultants and I had to make a decision: I withdrew from my statutory lecture schedule at Oxford.

We were new to one another. We had landed at Henderson Field on Guadalcanal in the Solomons. Even before we left Henderson Field for the capital, we were told how during World War II the marines had seized the airfield from the surprised Japanese as they were building it and driven them into the jungle. And as we approached Honiara, the ferocity of that distant campaign came dramatically into view. Stark wrecks of battleships, huge rusting tangles of iron, protruded eerily from the island's waters.

We were unlikely fellow travellers; Ian, a quiet, pleasant New Zealander; Peter, tall, good-looking Australian extrovert; Bob, swarthy, middle-aged, friendly American not lacking in confidence, our self-styled leader; and me. Bob, at the wheel of our hired station wagon, had arrived a day or two ahead of us and had got talking to Solomon Islanders at the bar of Honiara's Mendana Hotel. "These Solomon Islanders call our war against the Japanese a foreign invasion of their peaceful islands," he said, his eyes strained on the rough bush track. "We left behind thousands of war dead, their waters littered with destroyed battleships, and an arsenal of bombs and mortars on their lands. It was jungle fighting," he said.

Suddenly we had reached the Mendana for our first night's stay on Guadalcanal.

"That was more than thirty years ago," Peter resumed our earlier conversation as we assembled for dinner. "And now with the euphoria of independence of these islands from Colonial rule," he paused thoughtfully.

"The world has yet to respond to the Solomon Islanders' cry for a massive clean-up of this unwanted debris," Bob answered.

"The Japanese freighter Hurokawa was sunk with huge loss of life," added the hotel proprietor. "The worst of it is that its rusting remains are still polluting our beaches with oil spillage killing our fish."

Our time together was limited, for we were soon separating to visit different islands, but Ian and I had the pleasure of each other's company as far as Ghizo among the Shortland Islands west of Honiara. Again, we heard tales of ferocious battles which had been fought between divisions of New Zealand and American soldiers and the Japanese, of the allies leapfrogging from island to island.

It had come as a surprise to find so delightful a place for a night's stay, shrouded in tropical flowering shrubs of brilliant colours; but one story the proprietor had to tell over a drink at the bar was particularly sickening as he waved his hand toward an invisible island. "The world knows of the disastrous fall of Singapore," he said. "But who knows that the Japanese brought hundreds of British prisoners from Singapore right here to Ballalae, one of our small uninhabited islands. They were made to break hard rock for an airstrip. It was forced labour. Many died of fever or hunger. Many were beheaded and thrown into the sea."

With this disturbing backcloth of disaffection, Ian left for the villages and I was introduced to the oarsman of a rowing boat which, I was told, was the only means of reaching a group of women on Vonavona Island who had sent a message for me to visit. We set off early next morning, the boatman, to my surprise, using a single oar. It would take us a couple of hours rowing he thought; but the going was tediously slow when suddenly he cried: "Look!" and pointed to a small uninhabited island. "Jack Kennedy swam to that island when his battleship was torpedoed." In his excitement he let his oar slip. And it no longer mattered that a former President of the United States had survived being blown up by the Japanese only to be assassinated in his own country at the height of a brilliant presidency. We were adrift. In desperation we snatched at floating debris in the swirling water till by a miracle a large plank-like stick struck the side of the boat.

When at last Vonavona Island came into view, we were hailed by a group of young women gathered on the beach who were frantically waving as the boatman struggled with his makeshift oar to reach the shore.

But I had eyes for something else. Far in the distance along the empty coastline I had spotted a motorboat moored on the beach.

"The Solomons are a scattered archipelago of many islands," said the boatman as we chugged in open water. "Most of our people live in isolated settlements along the coasts."

Relieved when he had agreed to take me to one of the larger of these islands, I had joined the young women. They were from nearby islands on a course to learn more on growing vegetables. "We women have to grow all the food for the family," they said. "Men's work is cattle. We have to climb rocky paths a long way to our gardens." They pointed to the rugged terrain behind the beach. "It is hard work in the gardens with just our hoes and we have to carry everything on our backs."

"It's a new venture by the agriculture officers on Vella Lavella close by," said the boatman. "Don't know whether they are learning much but they are really enjoying themselves."

We were approaching Munda from where the boatman had said I could fly to Honiara on my way to the large and more populated Malaita Island. But just as we entered the bay into Munda, I was aghast to see that it was alive with crocodiles.

The boatman had laughed. "They won't tip my boat. They don't like the smells from the exhaust." Still, I didn't trust these huge mud-caked reptiles lurking in the bay and was utterly relieved when we had beached.

In Honiara I was joined by a Malaitan for the short flight to Auki, or rather the airstrip that served this provincial capital. This was no coincidence. Apparently he was to be with me throughout my stay on the island. "Malaitans," he said, "were deeply resentful of white people over an incident which occurred more than fifty years ago during Colonial rule. Bell, one of Britain's District Commissioners on Malaita, was murdered while collecting taxes. In retaliation the British imposed massive reprisals which are still vividly remembered to this day," he said.

It was a sobering introduction after the friendly engagements in Ghizo and on Vonavona Island in Western Province. Arriving in Auki, I was again warned of Malaitan hostility as we set out to visit some of the coastal settlements where feudalism, bride-price and tribal ceremonies had continued unchanged. And in complaint at the proliferation of foreign consultants who were turning up following independence, one field officer remarked: "Where did this idea come from that rural folk in feudal societies can be trained in five minutes like a sheepdog?"

"We Malaitans," said Auki officials, "did not suffer like the rest of our Solomon Island brethren from Japanese invasion during WW2." And I wondered as I returned to Honiara how the Japanese would have fared had they faced these volatile, hot-blooded, proud Malaitans.

Our departure from the Solomons for Sydney was imminent; we had met up again at the Mendana, each with a fascinating story to tell, four roving travellers who had been looking a little bit deeper into the country. And we were in holiday mood. Ian and Peter had decided to swim to a partially submerged Japanese wreck. Bob and I lazed chatting. That was Bob. Chatting.

In the event, it was our downfall as the three of us sat in the hired station wagon waiting for him to take the wheel. "Plenty of time," he had called. And when we finally left the hotel for our plane he had had to put his foot down on the accelerator. Suddenly, a motorcyclist shot out of a cross-road straight into the side of our vehicle. Instantly, even as we were all getting out, we were faced with four police officers, unaware that they had been following us.

"You are all under arrest," said the most senior officer. "Nationality?" he turned to Bob. "American," to Peter "Australian," to Ian "New

Zealand"; but he had paused, staring, without moving a muscle of his face, when I said "British". "You may go," he said, for no known reason.

At that moment, Ian jumped into the station wagon and drove like a maniac up a side road out of sight. And the police officers, as if anxious not to lose all of us, grabbed Bob, shoved him into their Land Rover and drove off.

Peter and I, left standing, started to walk. "If we miss our plane there's not another for a week," Peter said gloomily. But we were in luck. A passing vehicle gave us a lift. With take off imminent, we sprinted across the runway.

And there was Ian calmly boarding the plane.

We had been sponsored in the Solomons by the Asian Development Bank in Manila and changing planes in Sydney had been a bonus. Ian had alighted in Brisbane to visit a friend. While Peter and I spent a glorious evening dining at Australia's famous 'all fish' restaurant on Sydney Bay. As we started a five-course dinner with a dozen oysters and a fine glass of Australian wine, a fiery sun set over the Bay and little boats bobbed about with a myriad of dancing lights as darkness fell. Ian arrived next day and he and I went to Sydney's world famous Opera House designed by a Danish architect in the shape of a segmented orange, in the face of some opposition at his daring creation. There had been no news of Bob and we journeyed on without him.

Manila was on tight security. 'To all military personnel,' read the note on the glass panel of the Central Bank. 'Deposit your firearms with the security guard when transacting business inside the Bank.' Stone walls flanking the door had been scrawled with red paint 'Down with U.S.-Marcos. Long live NPA.' The New People's Army, military wing of the Philippine Communist Party, was expanding its rural and urban guerrilla war against the government. And it was Davao, capital of the southernmost province of Mindanao lying six hundred miles from Manila, that was haunting the government of President Marcos after seventeen years in power.

We had been placed in a heavily-guarded hotel in Manila's prosperous business quarter and were fetched and returned each day by an Asian Development Bank driver. I knew the Philippines well, and Mindanao in particular, and called to mind my last visit when hardly had I stepped from the plane in Manila than I had had an anonymous death threat. I thought of those anxious days, my escape to Davao city and eventual departure by a different route.

Today, in our hotel lounge, we were glued to the television listening to President Ferdinand Marcos address the nation. "Unless these killings abate," he said, "we will send more troops to these areas." Violence in the rugged Davao countryside I knew so well was now being mirrored by terrorism in Manila.

There had been a discreet silence from Asian Development Bank staff. But one night I persuaded the hotel security guards to allow a Filipino friend to visit; and we spoke in whispers fearing the walls might be bugged.

Who dared predict that President Marcos would be overthrown in a massive coup and suffer an ignoble death?

CHAPTER 18

PIG FAT AND CLAN WARFARE

Nothing had been heard of Bob, probably still languishing in the Solomons. Our write-up for the ADB in Manila finished, I had returned to England. I was to join an all-British team on a mission in Papua New Guinea. So it was back to the Pacific, and promised to be as exciting, as I flew out to Port Moresby. I entered the hotel bar on the night of my arrival as an Australian veteran of World War II was enthralling the crowded room with recollections of the ferocious fighting against a ruthless Japanese force and the shambles of their allied retreat across the rugged Owen Stanley Range.

"We were right here," he turned to a wall map, "fighting alongside a Papuan force on the slopes of the Owen Stanley mountain range. But the Japanese were heavily bunkered around Port Moresby and it took us weeks to flush them out and destroy them. It was the Japanese's first big defeat on land in the South Pacific," he raised a clenched fist, "the sweetest victory we had no time to celebrate because our boys were still fighting desperate battles across the water on Guadalcanal." He drained his tankard of local beer and called for another. Fellow Australians gathered round applauding loudly and it was hard to forget that Papua was no longer an Australian Protectorate.

But it had been a false start. Leave Port Moresby and fiery clansmen of Papua's 800 or so tribes peopled the provinces, and the heart of the nation throbbed.

I set off in a single-engine light aircraft piloted by an Australian to follow the trail of the Goilala living in a remote part of the Owen Stanley range. A tiny speck like a bird in infinite space, we flew over breathtaking mountain ranges, while the pilot searched for the hole in the cloud which would show him the grassy strip on the edge of a precipice. It was the only way in to Tapini and the rest house where I had hoped to meet up with a forest ranger.

As I was leaving Port Moresby, a New Zealand student in her gap year had come up begging me to take her on the flight and together we squeezed into the tiny aircraft. Suddenly the hole in the cloud obligingly appeared. The fantastically skilled pilot flew through it and touched down scarily on the lip of the precipice.

No sooner had we stepped from the plane than he swung round and flew off again before the hole in the cloud closed up. But not before he had said: "I will return in a week. Be ready. I won't wait. And if I don't find the hole in the cloud I'll turn back to Port Moresby."

Somewhat apprehensive, we found a travellers' rest house near the airstrip, an unlocked wooden building. Its empty shelves but for a partly filled bottle of Martini Rosso, discoloured and mildewed, suggested the place had had no recent visitors. But across the airstrip people were setting up a market stall and with this hopeful sign we went over and made purchases. Beyond, as far as the eye could see, was dense forest.

Suddenly, we heard the noise of a vehicle and to our utter relief the forest ranger I had been told to expect before we left Port Moresby, arrived.

Next day, he and I set off to villages hidden in the forest, while the New Zealand girl stayed around Tapini and the stall vendors.

Travelling across difficult terrain along water courses winding through dense forest, suddenly we emerged into a large open space and men sitting eating.

"We have stumbled on a pig feast," the forester said and would not approach. "Sacrifices for the dead ancestors, who knows?" He turned sharply and we moved away. All at once, we saw a large man savagely beating a woman with a heavy object.

I stopped, aghast, and the forester grabbed my arm and pulled us away.

"The woman is in terrible pain," I protested as we walked on. "You can see from her face. She must be about eight months pregnant."

"He's getting rid of the baby," the forester said, embarrassed. "It's the way they do things in these parts," he said, and quickly changed the subject.

We were about 27 km from Tapini airstrip and the forester waved an arm at the wall of forest which encircled the village he had called Tororo. "It may surprise you," he said, "the tribe in this mountain village has links with their *Wantok* as far away as the plains and the coast."

"Their *Wantok*?" I asked.

"It is a person's allegiance to their tribe or clan. The *Wantok* is paramount in clan warfare which has been going on for centuries. But personal allegiance to the tribe goes much further."

We had reached a wooden building, the size of a large shed, with the intricate network of *Wantok* still far from clear, to find a medical orderly the sole occupant. His scant shelf of first-aid stores was an odd touch of modern usage in a world of deeply-entrenched traditional life-styles.

Back in Tapini, we found the New Zealand girl at the open market store by the airstrip.

"These market people are clansmen, *Wantoks*, from Tororo village," the forester said. "They are packing vegetables from the village to put on the plane to Port Moresby. Besides this store, these Tororo sub-clans also have a small store in the city close by Koki market."

"Koki market?" I asked.

"The largest market in Port Moresby for fresh fruit and vegetables brought down from the mountain villages," the forester said.

He had not waited to see the plane arrive. "It all depends on the hole in the clouds," he had shrugged. "Sometimes the pilot has to turn back."

The New Zealand girl could not tear herself from the market store. I stayed by the airstrip, not keen to spend longer in these desolate mountains. Time passed. Still no break. It seemed that we were out of luck. Suddenly the clouds parted and there it was, a speck in the hole, then, like a winged bird, flying straight for the precipice and the tricky touchdown on the grassy strip behind.

The pilot was in a terrible hurry. The small hole in the clouds was already beginning to close. The vegetables had been rushed on board. But the New Zealand girl was still saying 'goodbye' at the market store. The pilot screamed from the cockpit, threatening to leave her behind. In sudden alarm, she dashed for the airstrip to be bundled into the light aircraft by a Tororo tribesman seconds before lift off.

"You're back," they cheered as I entered the bar of the Port Moresby hotel.

"We didn't tell you before you left," said a Brit. "The plane which took off for Tapini the week before yours crashed in the mountains. We hid the newspapers. Thought you might chicken out."

I saw the awesome Owen Stanley range in my mind's eye, that thrilling landing on the edge of a precipice. And I was glad they had not told.

And travelling from Port Moresby north across the coastal plains, there they were again, Tororo Goilala in scattered settlements, predatory strangers at flash points for rows between tribes on a whim.

Our pick-up truck had rattled along rough roads into Kairuku to meet a rival tribe. The warrior chief towered from a dais in front of a magnificent arched Papuan dwelling. Like a grand marshal he descended to our level. With a sweep of the hand he drew our attention to his new developments, housing with elaborate guttering to catch rainfall, loose hanging wires waiting to be connected. And then, he pointed to a grove of tall thin palms.

"Betel-nuts," he said, masticating one as he spoke, his mouth eaten away with a horrendous cancer from a long habit of chewing the stimulant. "Those Goilala migrants on our lands are looking for riches selling our betel-nuts," he went on. "We fight them with arrows."

And later, in the bar at the Port Moresby hotel, that same veteran Australian taking his nightly draught of beer, on hearing of our fascinating encounter, called: "They will feud over a trifling dispute. The clan's allegiance to *Wantok* is everything, the tradition is rock solid." With that, he gave a long whistle. "We Aussies have all but given up," he said.

Much later the Aussie's words were echoed in an article by Nick Squires, which appeared in the 'Telegraph' on 3 September, 2005, in which he wrote: "Clan warfare has raged for centuries but the introduction of powerful weapons has made the age old system of 'payback' far more deadly and made parts of the highlands utterly lawless. Feuds can last for months, even years, in a country in which allegiance to *Wantok* is paramount."

But for us, coming in from outside a few years earlier, it had been an electrifying, hugely engaging, experience we would not have missed.

CHAPTER 19

CLOSE SHAVE

It had been over forty years since the end of the Second World War and a new generation had taken over in Africa and Asia, bringing a fresh surge of energy. The old guard during the transition had been phased out; eager young men and women were coming forward like pilgrims celebrating deliverance. The 'European' had returned under a new guise – tourism had taken root, air travel had become commonplace.

And I was back in Africa, back in Sierra Leone where I had been before when the British had not long gone. It had seemed then that Sierra Leone's turbulent history was a thing of the past. This old British colony had been the 'dumping ground' for freed slaves from America, known as Creoles, who are still regarded as foreigners by some pagan tribes of the country. "The citizens of Freetown, the capital, are Africans who have little but their skins in common with this part of Africa where their ex-slave ancestors settled," wrote Lawrence Green in his story of the West African coast, *White Man's Grave*. "Every street in Freetown has its reminders of the slave days, its guns from slave ships embedded in the pavements… Upper-class Creoles are sending their children overseas for professional training; more humble families are settled in villages near the capital. Samuel Coleridge Taylor, composer of *Hiawatha*, who brought the spirit of Africa into his music, was the son of a Creole doctor of medicine from Freetown."

It is said that Sierra Leone had received its name, 'lion mountain', from early Portuguese adventurers who, on sailing into the country, saw what appeared to be an unmistakable impression of a lion's head and lion's rump – an image confirmed in their imagination by roars of thunder reverberating from steep wooded ravines. At this latter day, I had joined colleagues in a Land Rover on a perilous climb at the edge of a deep ravine for drinks at the invitation of Government overlooking the city; it was an exhilarating experience.

But it was on a rapid reconnaissance survey of the 'rural scene' across the country that I was primarily engaged; and with forty villages drawn from the national population census using a table of random numbers, I was joined by Wilfred, a citizen of Sierra Leone, to act as interpreter.

We set off to the villages in a station wagon along rough bush tracks isolated from towns and transport networks; and we were never quite sure where we would find somewhere to kip down for the night. A war with rebels of the Revolutionary United Front had been raging in the country since March 1991 and was particularly active as we moved ever closer into Sierra Leone's Northern Province; when we came upon a road worker laying down a road with the help of two British VSO volunteers, Robert and Calum. The road worker had a guest that night at the campsite but Calum had been away and was not due back till next morning and I was able to occupy his bed; Wilfred slept in our vehicle. Next morning we moved on to Gbindi village in our sample. It was very scary. The men were out fighting. Four or five women emerged from huts with menacing looks and set dogs on us. We made a hasty retreat. It was not till the next day that we heard the road project campsite had been ransacked less than an hour after we had left and that Robert and Calum had been taken hostage amid heavy exchanges of fire which had lasted for three hours. Wilfred and I had had a miraculous escape!

It was November 1994, and Robert and Calum had yet to experience the next five months in captivity – living on monkey and leaves, fantasising about home cooking, bouts of malaria ever present, boredom their worst enemy. Hardly were they safely back in London with their families than in a new surge of violence rebels had massacred anyone they came across at Koidu in the east of Freetown. It marked the third anniversary of the coup which brought Capt Valentine Strasser to power; and the war which had already claimed ten thousand lives.

Meanwhile, Wilfred and I had moved on to a remote part of the country in search of another village thrown up in our random sample. We had entered the extensive riverine area inhabited by the *black simulium fly,* the bites of which result in thousands of tiny worms living and breeding under the skin of the human population, invading the body and causing river blindness. So dense did we find the forest and bush that we had to abandon our station wagon and begin a long trek on foot in intense heat. We had passed through a settlement in a sudden clearing only to learn that we had to press on for another mile or so yet. The scene that confronted

Map of Sierra Leone.

us on our arrival was sad. Men in their prime, blinded by the fly, were being guided by a boy holding the end of a stick. No one comes here, they told us, which was brought home when a very old lady crept up and presented me with five tiny eggs. She is asking they said: "How is the King of England?" and we did not say he had been dead for almost half a century and that her country was no longer a British colony. They offered us wild palm wine which Wilfred declined and I cautiously tasted, while they told us of a sickness that was killing their children. "They wake up shouting and screaming in the night. In the morning they are dead," they said. It had been helpful that Kenyeh Barley had asked to travel with us on this journey, but she had been enjoying a mug full of palm wine and was resting in a hammock. She would not forget this 'lost village' when she was back in Freetown, she told the villagers through the haze of her heady wine.

It was later than we would have liked when we set off back through dense undergrowth accompanied for part of the way by one of the villagers. He was pointing to baboons balancing unsteadily on the tops of wild palm trees; while for us the going was hard and, feeling exhausted, I had wanted to rest on a rock when we reached the settlement. But Kenyeh and Wilfred were scared of the approaching dark. We still had quite a journey on foot before we would reach our vehicle – and I dare not lose sight of them in this forbidding jungle.

Kenyeh had gone back to Freetown. We had planned to stay over at Kenema in the east of the country. It was late, past 8 o'clock, when we arrived at the outskirts of the town; and here we were brought to a halt by a long line of stationary trucks. Ahead, we could see a dimly-lit military checkpoint. Our driver had panicked and rushed outside. He had not taken the ignition key and Wilfred and I did not get out. Suddenly, a policeman appeared in the moonlit sky and stared long and hard at the side of our vehicle. We said nothing, apprehensive, waited for him to speak and when he did we were astonished. He said: "You are from the Ministry. I will go tell the soldiers at the checkpoint to let you pass." He had misread the sign on our vehicle, 'Minster', for 'Ministry'.

Wilfred found our driver and we drove warily along the line of trucks to be startled at the checkpoint by a sudden blaze of floodlights on us as we passed through. Then the floodlights went out, leaving us to continue our dark and lonely drive into Kenema. That evening in a hostel in Kenema, we received a meal of field rat which had a kind of soft roe taste; and were told to keep the oil lamp alight all night to warn off intruders.

Our random sample of villages had taken us all over the country of this unhappy land. And yet? A spirit of optimism seemed to prevail.

Chapter 20

The Promise

I was about to celebrate my eightieth birthday and to 'call it a day'. The changing tides of a momentous century, through a Second World War, the demise of colonial empires, the creation of a commonwealth of nations, had been the legacy of our generation for a brighter future as a new century was a whisper away. But I had one more journey to make, one last visit to Jenyr in upriver Gambia, the village of my first arrival in Africa, when baboons and wild pig ravaged crops and maneless lions lurked in forest undergrowth. In the last half century this once small village had mirrored the upheavals and fortunes of much of Africa. It had been 1987, ten years ago, since Ebou and I had been back in Jenyr. At that time we had driven the ninety miles from the coast all the way on a new tarmac road through cheering villagers as we passed by. The Gambia at that date had enjoyed twenty years of independence; but a power struggle seemed to be sapping its energies.

Nonetheless, Jenyr villagers had greeted Ebou and I as always like family friends. It had only been when I walked across to the rice swamps behind the mangrove lining the river that I had had an awful shock: I had stood aghast! Before my eyes was a vast wasteland, salt pans, stagnant pools of acrid mud flats. And as I stared at this dreadful desolation, my mind flashed back a quarter-of-a century to 1962, when Ebou and I had visited Jenyr for the first time after our three-year sojourn in the village. Standing on this very spot then, I had seen a breathtaking carpet of ripening rice, golden panicles filled with grain swaying on the breeze. What had the villagers done in the 'free-fall' of the country's independence? I thought back to the time of independence. A new generation was taking over the affairs of the village, young men and women who had not had the benefit of advice and help from British agriculture and forest experts. Recklessly, they had ripped into the mangrove, torn down its branches for building materials they should have found elsewhere – and let the salt ravage the soil that once supplied their 'bread basket' in full measure.

On that heart-breaking day in 1987, Ebou and I knew that something had to be done. We had already sensed the village elders were not their usual selves. We drew the women together and suggested they turned to vegetable growing; and we agreed a suitable area in a single large rectangular plot, to be divided in parcels according to traditional hierarchies. Ebou and I would draw a plan. The men would help prepare the ground. We would arrange seed to be sent to the village on our return to Banjul. Then something happened that we did not foresee.

The day before we were due to leave, Ebou and I had been surprised that no one was around in the village except for a few children playing on the sandy village street. Strange, we thought, as a young man appeared, came up to us, and said: "You must follow me." We stepped forward. "Not you," he turned to Ebou, shaking his head. And we walked, I behind him, some distance through a tangle of bush obscuring our vision when suddenly we came to a clearing. And there they were, the Jenyr villagers in a packed semi-circle, the elders in the front, all grim-faced, not a smile. And a little distance away, facing the villagers, a chair had been placed. I was told to sit on the chair. And the villagers began to speak while a tall man at the back interpreted.

"You have written a book about us," they said. "What have you done for us?"

Here were the people I knew so well in every household, knew their fathers and mothers. It was like an inquisition. I had to reply and in that tense moment I saved a nerve-wracking situation with a flash of inspiration: "When I get back to England," I said, "I will find a village with people who will link with all of you in a spirit of friendship working together."

Today, ten years later in 1997, Jenyr was celebrating the successful outcome of that extraordinary gathering. The Yate-Genieri (Jenyr) Community Link had been born.

But Ebou and I were celebrating fifty years since our first arrival in Jenyr – 1947-1997. We would not come back again. And we were being feted – the drummers were vigorously beating their drums, the women were frantically dancing, everyone was singing at the top of their voices, stampeding the ground with their bare feet, raising clouds of dust in the dry sand. Ebou, now in his late seventies, was sitting on a platform high above the milling crowds like some ancient potentate, enjoying the spectacular performance. It would be some hours yet before the evening feasting and the giving of gifts. And I slipped away without anyone noticing. I called our driver and took the truck out of the village to a lonely spot about sixteen miles from Jenyr. I then left the truck and walked down to the river. I was quite alone in the fading light.

I had to say goodbye to this Africa which had been a heartbeat of my life. I gazed across the still waters of the mighty Gambia lapping at my feet where nothing stirred to unmask its deep secrets – its terrible share in the evil shipment of slaves to the Americas, the white explorers in search of the Niger who never returned, the latter day *Lady Wright,* 'the Governor's ship', which sailed like royalty in a magical blaze of fairy lights in the dark of the night, the fishermen in their dugouts. As I stood alone, the setting sun turned red across the sky and ripples of gold danced upon the silent waters.